BLACKJACK FOR WINNERS

BLACKJACK FOR WINNERS

by
Scott Frank

BARRICADE BOOKS INC.
FORT LEE, NEW JERSEY

Published by Barricade Books Inc.
1530 Palisade Avenue
Fort Lee, NJ 07024

Distributed by Publishers Group West
4065 Hollis
Emeryville, CA 94608

Printed in the United States of America.

Library of Congress Cataloging-in-Publication Data

Frank, Scott, 1950–
    Blackjack for winners/Scott Frank.
        p.   cm.
    ISBN 0-942637-88-7 : $11.95
    1. Blackjack (Game) I. Title.
    GV1295.B55F73   1993
    795.42—dc20   92–39821
                                        CIP

0 9 8 7 6 5 4 3 2 1

My grateful thanks to Katie Killary. Her moral and material support have gone a long way towards making this book possible.

Table of Contents

Introduction   3

1. A Background of the Game and Its Systems   7
2. Exploding Superstitions   11

    Myth #1: The Insidious Myth of Basic
           Strategy   12

    Myth #2: Tens and Aces Are the Most
           Important Cards   16

    Myth #3: Breaking Is Always Bad! (Or:
           There's Nothing To Be Gained
           From Losing)   19

    Myth #4: Bet Up When You're Winning   21

3. The Core System   23

    The Balanced Deck: Accidents Will
      Happen!   27

    The Influence of the Heavy Core   29

    The Influence of the Light Core   35

4. Blackjack is a Fluid Game (How To Adjust
   Your Play From the First Cards Dealt)   39
5. Tracking the Core Ratio   55
6. Cashing In On a Core Meltdown   69
7. Core Training   73
8. Betting and Bankroll   87
9. Core Discipline (Manners At the Table)   97

    How Counters Give Themselves Away   97

    The Pit Boss   98

    Drinking   101

Breathing   102
The Double Down Card   102
Tipping the Dealer   103
10. Casino Defenses or Casino Cheating?   105
Deck Stacking   107
Shills   108
Pressure On Dealers To Win   108
Picking the Deck   109
Stripping the Deck   110
The Mechanic   110
Dealing Seconds   112
The Amateur Mechanic   114
11. Six Ways To Improve Your Game Before You
    Even Sit Down (Or: How To Find A Good
    Table)   117
APPENDIX A: Core Strategy Charts
    Hitting   122
    Hard Doubles   123
    Soft Doubles   124
    Splitting   125
APPENDIX B: Surrender and Insurance   127
APPENDIX C: Dealer Final Total
    Probabilities (When Dealer Doesn't Have
    Blackjack)   131
GLOSSARY   133

Upon winning the World,
Great Alexander wept
For then he realized
That there was Nothing left.

Introduction

There are 10^{68} ways (one followed by 68 zeros) for the 52 cards of the deck to be ordered. But, merely because there are more ways to stack a deck than there are atoms in the entire Earth combined with the total number of seconds elapsed since the Big Bang, you needn't be discouraged from winning at Blackjack. Some of the new casino defenses, however, may be quite discouraging. What with new shuffles, card clumping, post-play card pick-up techniques, rules variations, shills and mechanics (saboteur players and cheating dealers for the casino), even the most adept Plus/Minus Ten Counters, Shuffle Trackers and Systems Players are finding that they're having less success than the Hunch Player.

Over the past three years I've developed from a run-of-the-mill (i.e., losing) blackjack player into an expert who wins at four of every five sittings. I owe my success to a simple and quite revolutionary strategy which I call the CORE System.

I devised the CORE System after taking yet another class on combating casino defenses. After suffering through three days of what the strident instructor proudly referred to as "Blackjack Bootcamp" (and paying $495 for that dubious privilege), I was handed a line about seeking out neutral and dealer biased tables and told to be willing to risk twelve betting units.

What? Isn't that a description of how I used to play blackjack *before* I started studying systems and courses? So, I realized, the leading blackjack specialists, the very gurus of the game, are really back at square one. The casinos have beaten them. But, in my angry frustration at being taken for $495, I devised a new and important concept.

I discovered that a blackjack deck has a Core in it, which I'm going to identify for you, and which, as it fluctuates between light (or hollow) to heavy (or dense), predictably alters the conditions of the game—including the so-called "flukes" of the deck which have previously been given over to chance. Blackjack will become a game of skill for you, as it is for me. For, while the game contains a measure of luck, the majority of it has been mathematically analyzed, often to within one thousandth of one percent (.001%).

With my mathematically sound system, you will be taught tip-off signs that indicate when advantage has swung to your favor. You will learn to differentiate between types of losing hands, providing further signposts as the game progresses.

To say that the "Core of the deck" controls the game is like saying the steering wheel controls a car. When you hop into your car there are many important factors to consider in order to arrive safely at your destination, but the steering wheel will almost always be the overriding factor in determining what direction your trip takes.

The CORE System, with its new strategies, actually flourishes against today's casino defenses. It is the most revolutionary style of play to arise since Dr. Edward Thorp introduced his Plus/Minus Ten Counting System in the early sixties. His system is now obsolete.

The mathematics in this book are documented from the works of the three leading math authorities of the game: Dr. Peter Griffin, of California State University at Sacramento *(The Theory of Blackjack,* Huntington

Press, 1988 ed.), Julian Braun *(How To Play Winning Blackjack*, Data House Publishing, 1980) and Dr. Edward Thorp, whose *Beat the Dealer* is still a solid source of blackjack mathematics, despite the antiquation of his Ten Counting System. I recommend all of these sources if you want to confirm or explore the math of the CORE System, or of the game in general.

Chapter 1.

A Background of the Game and Its Systems

Blackjack is a simple game. Object and play are elementary. The problems that we encounter while playing it are simple, and so should be the answers.

Up until the early Sixties accepted styles of play included standard strategies such as "mimic the dealer" (stand on seventeen or more; hit sixteen or less; no doubling or splitting). Others insisted that one should never hit a sixteen against Dealer's ten, for that was courting certain death. Most of these styles favored the house.

In the early Sixties a mathematician, Dr. Edward O. Thorp, devised a method of tracking the ten-valued cards and the aces. He used a plus/minus counting system (cards two thru six = +1; seven thru nine = 0; ten thru ace = −1), a brilliantly simple solution for tracking the cards which he considered the most important. He then combined it with a computer-based strategy that called for the most favorable response to each possible situation.

His system was very successful. In fact, it single-handedly caused Las Vegas to make rule alterations. During 1964, for a brief period, the Las Vegas Hotel Resort Association announced that the rules of blackjack were being changed. No longer would they allow the splitting of aces, and doubling down was limited to hard eleven. Said spokesman Gabriel Vogliatti, "In the last fifteen years there hasn't been one plane that landed without at least one person in the possession of a system. This guy (meaning Thorp) is the first in Las Vegas history to have a system that works."

It was only a matter of weeks, what with dropping tourism rates and screaming dealers, who were losing tips, before they reverted to the original rules. After all, the good players just continued to win, though not quite as much, and the bad players just stopped playing.

Much of casino blackjack history from that point until now has been the assault of the Ten Counters and the efforts of the casinos to deal with them. The War Of The Tens. For a while, this consisted of merely throwing out anyone suspected of counting, and, in some places, just to be on the safe side, throwing out anyone who was winning.

Then a counting superstar, Ken Uston, successfully sued the Atlantic City casinos for discriminating against counters. Facing the same case in Nevada, however, the courts, while not going so far as to declare counting illegal (as most dealers and pit bosses will claim), did uphold the right of the resort industry to protect itself when its livelihood was threatened. In other words, the Nevada casinos can still bar counters.

Still, despite this huge difference in attitudes between the two states, they faced an identical problem: how to defeat the Counter. Because of the New Jersey Supreme Court ruling, eastern casinos had to find non-expulsion methods to combat them.

First, Atlantic City did away with most of their one- and two-deck games, creating four-, six- and eight-deck "shoes." Then they worked on their shuffles and post-play card pick-up techniques, those which encouraged extreme clumping in the decks or shoes. [Clump: a group of cards of similar or like value bunched in one area of the deck.] These clumps of tens and small cards led to distorted, inflated counts, effectively stymieing the counters. The new defenses rapidly spread west, to Nevada. If you haven't experienced the new clumping, you're in for a shock.

What the casinos have done with their defenses is very effective and, really, quite brilliant. Tired of making it easy for the Ten Counters, they didn't want their defenses to ruin the game for everyone else. So, while barely altering the motions of play, they devised a defense that both increases their take and defeats the Ten Counter.

Dealers still shuffle the same amount of time, some-times even less, using shuffles that preserve the struc-ture of the deck. All of the cards remain on the table until the end of play, taking up less time for card pick-up and allowing them to preserve trends in the deck. For instance, if the cards have been coming out high/low/high/low (really just a clump of highs mixed with a clump of lows) and they're returned to the deck in the same order, they're likely to come out again in similar fashion. Clumps of cards tend to survive four, five and even more rounds of play. And the casinos noticed that in new, unshuffled decks there are ready-made clumps of tens and small-valued cards. They figured that if the Ten Counters want tens, then let 'em drown in them.

Inflated ten counts started to appear. The Counters, drooling with anticipation, would plop down their heavy bets, only to see more small cards come out. And when the paint finally showed, everybody got some, so they all pushed twenty with the dealer. These days the Counter does no better, sometimes worse, than the Hunch Player.

The casinos know one other thing: Some player will always find a mathematical way to beat them.

Chapter 2.

Exploding Superstitions

There are some important facts and statistics to consider before I introduce the CORE System. You, the player, in order to keep up with the casinos, must be open to new points of view and new strategies. The casinos certainly take this attitude as they successfully search for defenses against sharp players and new systems. There is no "right way" to play blackjack. What's right at one table may rapidly wipe you out at the next. The game is a fluid, dynamic situation which will inevitably be victorious over anyone who tries to approach it with rigidity.

Some people get around this by sitting only at tables that look like they'll accommodate their personal method of play. They often spend much time scouting, sometimes finding nothing suitable in a particular casino. When they finally do find the "right" table, they may be limited to only four or five hands before conditions deteriorate and they leave. While the success rate of these players may look impressive on paper, in reality they are limited to winnings of about one to four hands per "scouting hour"—not very satisfying, unless they're betting a large amount per hand. They get in very little playing time, endlessly looking for that "Home Run Table", that big win streak, hoping desperately that they'll find it before their discipline breaks down or their vacation ends.

Many systems players have the complaint that their system, while it works, takes all the fun out of the game. Mathematician Julian Braun, author of one of the first practical computer Basic Strategies, wrote in his book, *How To Play Winning Blackjack*: "Winning at blackjack demands a game plan. Something you can believe in and be guided by. Basic Strategy is at the foundation of it all. You must adhere to it strictly, deviating not at all. Your moves must be as mechanical as those of the Dealer."

Does this sound like fun? Something you'd care to spend your vacation doing? The truth is that few people have the will or desire to become a blackjack machine. And so, we will explore the first, and possibly, the most insidious superstition of blackjack.

MYTH #1: THE INSIDIOUS MYTH OF BASIC STRATEGY

Games such as craps or roulette are examples of the "Law Of Independent Trials"; whatever number comes up during one play is not going to affect what number appears on the following play. Blackjack does not follow this law. The course taken by a deck or shoe is greatly dependent upon what cards have been previously depleted from it. Add the effects of shuffles, cuts and post-play card pick-up techniques, and blackjack begins to look tantalizingly like a game that might somehow be tracked (and stacked).

Tempted by this concept, some mathematicians of the Fifties and Sixties put all of the various player/dealer hand combinations into a computer and had it play out millions of hands to determine, to the thousandth's (.001) place, what the "correct," or most advantageous move is for every situation, given a random deck.

The key phrase here is "given a random deck." Just what is this random deck? In statistics, the word "random" refers to a set of things, any of which has an equal chance of occurring. The mathematicians knew that the "Basic Strategy" they were offering had limited validity, because any deck's possibilities change as soon as some cards are dealt out. And they were quite aware that different casinos had different shuffling techniques, some producing anything but a random deck. Furthermore, a new deck is always set up the same way. Take a look at one—it will show you a lot. At what point does that new deck, chock full of card clumps, become the much touted random deck? It will most likely be replaced by the pit boss hours before it shows any signs of being random.

But this hasn't stopped veritable armies of players who, for the last three decades, have been barrelling on with Basic Strategy, faithfully bulling their way through decks and shoes with consistent play from beginning to end, coolly holding their heads aloft those that hadn't the "smarts" to follow the seemingly "indisputable" evidence presented by a billion computer-played hands. A lot of those players could remember only half of the Basic Strategy charts that they'd xeroxed and covertly carried into their hotel rooms, but they still held that they must be that much more skilled than the regular, uneducated player.

Basic Strategy has so insidiously worked its way into blackjack lore that some people actually equate it with the rules of the game. I recount a conversation between a basic strategist (B.S.) and me:

B.S.: "I took a class on blackjack in college."

Me: "You mean that they taught you how to track cards, the dealer possibilities, counting, etc?"

B.S.: "No, but they taught me how to play. You know, the right moves to make—the Basic Strategy."

Basic Strategy is actually taught in college as "The Way To Play Blackjack!"

Now, this Basic Strategy, played consistently from the beginning to the end of a deck, will usually not be enough to allow you to become a winning player. All Basic Strategy is saying is that if you played head-to-head with a dealer, and she shuffled up each time after dealing a hand to you, and you played a thousand or ten thousand hands like that, by following Basic Strategy, you may have (depending on house rules) a slight edge over the dealer.

But, in real life, almost any time that more than four cards are dealt out, a bias of some sort has developed in the deck as the result of the depletion of certain card values. Sometimes that bias will react favorably to Basic Strategy, and about an equal amount of time it won't. A minority of the time, the deck will retain enough balance to have no bias after the first few hands, but, by and large, it will be altered enough to cause the blanket use of Basic Strategy over months and years to be as successful as flipping a coin and always calling heads.

The use of Basic Strategy, in certain situations, is one way that pit bosses detect counters. Generally, though, they don't care about it because most users don't get very sophisticated in their play—they just memorize some charts and respond accordingly. The casinos have devised some very successful defenses against Basic Strategy, so, on the whole, they don't mind seeing it.

The reason for these defenses is that some Basic

Strategy players realized that the simple charts weren't enough to win. These players learned the other half of Thorp's system: the plus/minus method of tracking tens and aces. It was brilliant in its simplicity:

$$\text{Cards } 2\text{-}6 \ = \ +1$$
$$\text{Cards } 7\text{-}9 \ = \ 0$$
$$\text{Cards } 10\text{-A} \ = \ -1$$

By keeping count of the pluses and minuses, they could tell when the deck contained depletions and accumulations of Tens and Aces. A +6 count meant simply that the remaining deck contained six extra tens or aces than a normal deck of that size would. Extra tens or aces were interpreted as good, their depletion was bad.

The advanced counters could take their current numbers and refer back to their Advanced Basic Strategy charts, which would tell them how to change their moves in response to the new bias in the remaining deck. If they lost the hand anyway, they referred to "bad deck integrity" and chalked it up to misfortune. The line between "deck integrity" and luck is very obscure. "Deck integrity" and "unfavorable bias" became catch-all phrases to explain the many facets of the game which still seemed to be determined by mere chance. With the CORE System you'll learn how to predict much of this so-called "luck."

A normal deck has a ten density of about 31%, that is, 31% of the cards are tens. Ideal ten density, the percentage at which Basic Strategy supposedly functions at its best, is held as being 41%. Normal dealer bust probability is 28.36% (according to Thorp). When ideal ten density, 41%, is achieved, dealer bust probability rises up to only about 29.5%—barely a 1% improvement! For players who continually yearn for the dealer to bust these are sobering statistics.

Another, more obvious drawback to the Thorp Plus/Minus System is that it equates in importance the seven and the nine, counting them both as zero. This is a serious mistake for any player to make.

But the biggest weakness in any Ten Counting System is an assumption that brings us to our second superstition.

MYTH #2: TENS AND ACES ARE THE MOST IMPORTANT CARDS

Thorp chose the ten to track, not only for its high value, but because there are sixteen in each deck, compared to just four cards of every other value. This, he reasoned, makes it the most important card. But was he correct?

The most outstanding change in blackjack today is the Plus/Minus Ten Counting System's inability to win. The new clumping and shuffling has led to large, distorted counts, and the losses of the large bets that often go with these counts. Here are the three main scenarios that confront today's card counters:

Scenario #1: The Ten Counter has found a shoe that has a third of its tens clumped in one small part of it. A seemingly endless stream of low cards (two thru nine) have come out and the count has zoomed sky-high. He raises his bet, but out come more little cards. He loses large bets. Finally, he reaches the long-awaited +22 vein of gold—and what happens? Everyone gets dealt a twenty, including the dealer, and they all push (tie). All the tens are used up.

Scenario #2: A clump of tens has been mixed in with a clump of low- or middle-range cards. The count is high and the Counter raises his bet. Everyone gets dealt a stiff (hard twelve thru sixteen), with the dealer showing a ten. Basic Strategy compels them to take hits. The counter and most everyone else bust out, dealer turns over a sixteen, hits with a queen to bust, but most everyone's already lost. Then the dealer carefully picks up the cards in order. All those stiffs are available for the next go-round.

Scenario #3: Dealer finally shows a low card (two thru six), but our Counter's dealt a low, possibly, a very low hand. He takes hits until he reaches a stiff total, then, according to Basic Strategy, he stops. Heck, let the dealer bust instead! Dealer turns over another low card, total, maybe eight or nine, and proceeds to hit it with two or three or four more little cards, ending up with one of those gut-wrenching standing hands, wiping out all the stiffs. The deck was in a small clump at the time.

These are the three scenarios most commonly encountered when you play in a casino that has adopted some form of the Defensive Deck. Even the so-called Advanced Counting Systems, most notably by Lawrence Revere and Stanford Wong, offering confusing spectrums of different values for each denomination of the deck, all magically adding up to zero, will make no difference in the above scenarios. (There is a fantastic array of these systems, such as two $= 67$; three $= 93$; four $= 132$; ten $= -180$, etc. The most memorable to me is one that has ace thru nine $= +4$ and ten $= -9$.)

But the truth is that long before the heavy clumping started, many counters were complaining that too many times were they getting high counts and still losing.

Besides, they added, they went on "unexplainable" winning streaks during marked negative counts. Naturally, they had out only the minimum bet during those streaks. Rather than seek some logical explanation for these happenings, they were just assigned to the "flukes of the game," "deck integrity," luck, or "unfavorable biases," as you may have it. A lot of these quirks, as we'll see, can be explained by the density of the deck's Core.

Really, no matter what the casinos throw at you, the desirability of the ten has been highly overrated. A player can win a hand many different ways without even seeing a ten. And tens are really only good for the player about half of the time that they appear, that is, when combined with a second card, or cards, comprising a high value (8,9,T,A), or when hitting double downs (hard only) and with the high splits (8,8; 9,9; T,T; A,A). Almost half the deck (2,3,4,5,6,7) won't sit well with ten; for most soft doubles they are uneventful, or even bad.

It's a mistake to ignore the lower half of the deck. It's also a weak plan to put too much stress on the hope of the dealer's bust probability. Consider these basic statistics:

DEALER'S OVERALL BUST PROBABILITY: 28.36%

Dlr. Up Card:	A	2	3	4	5	6	7	8	9	T
Chance of Bust:	11.65%	35.30%	37.56%	40.28%	42.89%	42.08%	25.99%	23.86%	23.34%	21.43%

Depending on a dealer bust is clearly not a profitable strategy in the long run. Even when she is showing a five or six, she has less than a 50% chance of busting.

DEALER'S FINAL TOTAL PROBABILITIES
[Stand on Soft 17]

17	18	19	20	21	Nat. BJ	Bust
14.58%	13.81%	13.48%	17.58%	7.36%	4.83%	28.36%

The most common dealer hand is twenty, followed by seventeen. Dealer will end up with a standing total of eighteen or better over 57% of the time.

PLAYER'S EXPECTATION OF WINNING, DEPENDING ON PLAYER'S TOTAL

17 or less	18	19	20	21	Nat. BJ	[BJ occurs about once every 21 hands. One
28.36%	42.94%	56.75%	70.23%	87.81%	95.17%	BJ in 21 you will push with the Dealer.]

You must have a nineteen or better to have more than a 50/50 chance of winning!

The Ten Tracking System, and any system like it, which depends on the combination of Dealer Busts (28.36% of the time) and the chances of being dealt high hands (i.e., nineteen and over), is clearly a tenuous plan at best. You'll be dealt a nineteen or above on your first two cards only about 21% of the time—about once every five hands. On the other hand, you're going to be dealt hard twelve thru eighteen about 47.5% of the time*; the hard stiffs, twelve thru sixteen, 36.8% of all two-card hands!**

The way that the sellers of Ten Counting Systems attempt to withstand these horrifying statistics is by advising practitioners to avoid breaking and losing tables. Thus, we arrive at our third superstition.

MYTH #3: BREAKING IS ALWAYS BAD!
(Or: There's Nothing To Be Gained From Losing)

Most blackjack gurus teach that if you break twice in a row, or two out of three times, to run, not walk, from the table. From their standpoint, you inevitably lose your bet

---

*This doesn't include 6,6; 7,7; 8,8; 9,9. These occur another 2.2% of the time, or about .55% each

**Again, this doesn't include 6,6; 7,7; 8,8.

when you bust out, and losing is losing, no matter how you spell it.

While you may lose your money when the dealer bests you or you bust, and though it may be discouraging to watch general breaking activity increase around you, as a CORE Player you will learn to distinguish between the different types of losing. For there's a wealth of information to be gained by observing the manner of loss taking place.

Were you beaten by a higher hand? Did you bust outright, before the hand was over? Did you lose on a double down? If you did bust out, was it on twelve, thirteen or fourteen, or was it on fifteen or sixteen? Did the dealer bust after you did? All of these things have implications that you must consider if you want to get a handle on what's really happening in front of you.

What if I offered you this deal? I'll give you a better chance to be dealt a nineteen, twenty or BJ. Included in this offer is a higher probability of getting a nine or a ten if you double down. The only thing that you would have to agree on is to tolerate a higher chance of busting as your means of losing. (Not a much higher chance of losing—just more busts as the means of loss.) Wouldn't you want that trade-off? The advantages obviously outweigh the disadvantages! The CORE System is going to show you how to make that trade!

There is one more superstition which we must explore before we get to the heart of the matter. It's in the area of money management. One of the advantages of most gambling games is that you don't always have to win a majority of your bets in order to come out ahead, because you can vary the size of those bets. So, let's explore the last myth.

MYTH #4: BET UP WHEN YOU'RE WINNING

This philosophy, and its counterpart, "Don't Chase Your Bets," are the two trains of thought that keep most people's winning sessions within reasonable bounds, from the casino's viewpoint.

Of course, the most effective betting pattern, by far, is one which raises bets when a strategic advantage is perceived. Betting up when you see that the game is in your favor, staying conservative when you see that it's not, or when it's merely neutral. But most people don't perceive these trends; their betting is mostly a simple, immediate response to what happened to them the preceding hand, or just on hunch.

When physicist Albert Einstein was asked for a sure winning method for the game of roulette, he responded that, though there's no sure method, the simplest, surest way is to double up on losses. Of course, this idea is easily applied to other games.

The casinos know this; that's why we see table limits on betting amounts. Furthermore, most people's bankrolls don't permit them to pursue this line.

Frank Barstow, a gaming mathematician, has written: "The up-as-you-win method accounts for nearly all the big killings in casino gambling, but it is a major, if not *the* major contributor to casino profits." The disadvantage of the up-as-you win style is that it's possible to win more hands than you lose in a given period and still end up a monetary loser. Imagine this sequence: bet 1, win; bet 2, win; bet 3 win; bet 5, lose; bet 3, lose. You've won three hands and lost two, but you're behind -2. Add some double downs and/or splits to the losses and you're even worse off.

The opposite of this, betting up on losses, if played no matter how lousy the game is, will very probably lead to disaster. But, as Barstow points out, with some prudence and discipline, the up-on-losses method "is unquestionably one of the surest ways to win."

With both Einstein and Barstow supporting a limited, controlled up-on-losses method, we should probably give it some consideration. After all, it means that you can end up ahead even though you've lost more hands than you've won. But, as I've mentioned before, and mathematician Peter Griffin has demonstrated, the best money management method is one that stays conservative during periods of disadvantage and raises during times of strategic advantage. That is one basis of every *successful* blackjack system, including the CORE System. You're going to learn how to recognize those times of strategic advantage.

And, as far as myths go, this is probably a good time to make one last point.

Casinos want you to internalize your failures. They want you to blame your "stupidity" or "irresponsibility" when you lose. When you win, they want you to feel that you didn't bet enough—that, if you were "smarter" you would've made bigger bets.

My advice to you is don't spend time dwelling on the past. Forget the "what-ifs" and "if onlys." Some of you may have already run into this state of mind: the bettor that starts to feel a sense of loss when they win and a feeling of not doing so bad when they lose. If *you* find yourself thinking like this, it means that it's time for you to take a break and regroup, because the casino has gotten its hook into you and is just reeling you in.

Chapter 3.

The Core System

Herein are enclosed the tables and charts for the CORE System.

The trick that any systems player must master is combining the "frozen moments" presented in strategy charts with the "fluid" game that blackjack really is.

This sense of fluidity is an appropriate way to describe play. Even the best players, at the moments that they're at the top of their game, are aware only of the "trends" of the deck, and what the possibilities of the moment are.

An assured, easy confidence is that state of mind which we want to achieve. This is how we'll utilize the CORE System to its max: with *RELAXED VIGILANCE.*

TABLE #1

Second Card

	2	3	4	5	6	7	8	9	10	10	10	10	A
2	4	5	6	7	8	9	10	11	12	12	12	12	3/13
3	5	6	7	8	9	10	11	12	13	13	13	13	4/14
4	6	7	8	9	10	11	12	13	14	14	14	14	5/15
5	7	8	9	X	X	X	X	14	15	15	15	15	6/16
6	8	9	10	X	X	X	X	15	16	16	16	16	7/17
7	9	10	11	X	X	X	X	16	17	17	17	17	8/18
8	10	11	12	X	X	X	X	17	18	18	18	18	9/19
9	11	12	13	14	15	16	17	18	19	19	19	19	10/20
10	12	13	14	15	16	17	18	19	20	20	20	20	BJ
10	12	13	14	15	16	17	18	19	20	20	20	20	BJ
10	12	13	14	15	16	17	18	19	20	20	20	20	BJ
10	12	13	14	15	16	17	18	19	20	20	20	20	BJ
A	3/13	4/14	5/15	6/16	7/17	8/18	9/19	10/20	BJ	BJ	BJ	BJ	2/20

First Card

As the chart in Table #1 shows, there are 169 possible two-card combinations, for the player or dealer to be dealt. At this point, the odds of receiving any particular hand are virtually the same for the dealer as they are for the player. The dealer reveals only one card, though, and the first decisions and actions will have to be taken by the players.

The most common two-card hand which you'll receive is twenty, which comes out 10.6% of the time. (I'm including soft twenty (A,9), on which you should never double down. Twenty is the only hand for which the percentages for soft and hard hands will be combined. In all other cases, soft and hard figures will be kept separate.) That big block of 19s, 20s and BJs in the lower right hand quadrant may look substantial and tempting to you, but here is the actual breakdown of the hand values and the percentage of times that you can expect to have them dealt to you on your first two cards:

4,5,6,7,8 =	8.8% (15)	possible combinations
Hard Dbls. 9,10,11 =	12.5% (21)	
Hard 12, 13, 14 =	24.9% (42)	
Hard 15 + 16 =	13.6% (23)	
Hard 12 thru 16 =	38.5% (65)	
Hard 17 & 18 =	11.2% (19)	
Hard 15 thru 18 =	24.9% (42)	
Hard 12 thru 18 =	49.7% (84)	
Hard 19 =	4.7% (8)	
20 (incl. A,9) =	10.6% (18)	
Blackjack (21) =	4.7% (8)	[or, roughly, once in every 21 hands.]
Hard 19 thru 21 =	20.1% (34)	
Soft Hands (not incl. A,A;A,9;BJ) =	8.3% (14)	

You'll also notice two vertical and two horizontal lines outlining the region influenced by the cards 5,6,7,8. These four cards will heretofore be known as "The Core Cards." One of the advantages of the CORE System is that you have to track only four card values. The traditional Thorp system, and almost all others, involve tracking eight or more card values. This is one reason why clumping so effectively defeats them. The Core Cards, 5,6,7,8, also have the advantage of being consecutive in value, so it's not unusual to find clumps that contain two or more Core values in any deck or shoe.

Let's run through the list of figures above and you'll see why I've grouped some of them in the repetitive manner that I have.

Of the 169 possible two-card hands, fifteen total eight or below (8.8%). They don't play a big part in the game, except, possibly, the two sets of pairs that you may split (2,2; 3,3), and, occasionally, the total eight, on which some daredevil may double down.

One-eighth of your hard hands offer reasonably safe potential for doubling down (9, 10, 11), providing that the house allows it on something other than just ten and eleven. Nineteen of the twenty-one hard doubles are contained inside the Core boundaries. That's 91% of them.

Almost four of every ten hands you'll be dealt will be stiffs (twelve thru sixteen: sixty-five of 169 (38.5%). Of these, thirty-seven of sixty-five of them are constructed of at least one Core card (57%).

Of the two-card fifteens through eighteens, there are forty-two. Fully forty-one of these forty-two (97.6%) are made of at least one Core card. Remember: You will lose or push (tie) 57.06% of all hands eighteen or under.

Eight of every ten two-card deals will be eighteen or under. More startling is the fact that you'll lose any hand of sixteen or less 71.64% of the time! Three of every five deals will be sixteen or under.

Specifically, the figures for Core card (five thru eight) involvement are:

Hard Doubles 9,10,11 = 91% (19 of 21)
Hard Stiffs 12 thru 16 = 56.9% (37 of 65)
Low, Hard Standing Hands 17 & 18 = 94.7% (18 of 19)
Soft Hands A,2–A,8 = 57.1% (8 of 14)
Pairs (not incl. T,T; 4,4; 5,5 = 42.9% (the 6,6; 7,7; 8,8)
These are never split.)

Core cards make up 52% (88 of 169) of the two-card hands you will be dealt.

I divide the types of hands into two broad categories: the Standing Hands, which play themselves, and the Active Hands—hands which demand a decision on whether to hit or stand. One of the disadvantages of tracking tens is that they are involved in a greater percentage of Standing Hands, which give you no say in your own fate, than are Core cards. It's the 116 Active Hands that make or break your game—those wily stiffs and risky double downs. And the Core cards are part of fully 68 of those 116 hands, or 61.3%!

The boundaries formed by the crossing lines on Table #1 seem to form a core on the chart, and, in a very real sense, the cards 5,6,7,8 can be said to form the "Core of the deck."

Let's look at another aspect of the Core. As the cards five through eight are depleted from the deck:

   –the frequency of two-card 7s thru 18s is *somewhat reduced.*

   –the frequency of two-card 10s thru 16 is *reduced a bit more.*

   –the amount of two-card 12s thru 14s is *reduced considerably!*

And it is logical to expect an increase in activity in the areas of the chart that aren't part of the depleted 5-8 Core boundaries. This includes that meaty lower right-hand corner holding thirty of the thirty-two nineteens, twenties and blackjacks.

Furthermore, with Core depletion, those Dealer twelves thru sixteens will be less likely to be hit by a five, six, seven or eight, leading to more dealer busts!

In a very real sense, the game of blackjack can be said to revolve around the 5-8 Core contained in every deck.

But we've only been looking at one side of the picture. The following charts (Table #2) will outline the hallmarks and characteristics of the two different types of Cores—the Heavy (or Dense) Core and the Light (or Hollow) Core.

THE BALANCED DECK: ACCIDENTS WILL HAPPEN!

There are really three types of games that you'll encounter when using the CORE System. The first is the least common: the game with a balanced deck. As long as the deck remains fairly well distributed and balanced, the traditional Basic Strategy as devised by Thorp and Braun is the appropriate way to play your hands. However, even by Thorp's own calculations, if you are dealing with a balanced, or random deck, it will develop a bias one way or the other over half the time as soon as 20% of the

TABLE #2

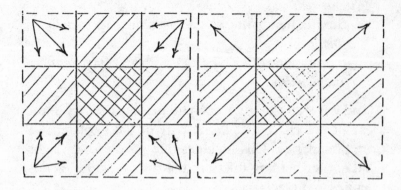

HEAVY (DENSE) CORE	LIGHT (HOLLOW) CORE
—Slow, laborious game	—More active, livelier game
—More two-card 15s, 16s, 17s, 18s	—More 19s, 20s, BJs
—More DD opportunities; many take bad hits.	—Less DD opportunities but better hits on them.
—Dealer makes more Standing Hands	—Dealer busts her Stiffs more
—less busting activity overall	—More busting activity overall
—12s, 13s, 14s take more successful hits.	—Player 12s, 13s, 14s hit less successfully
—Few Blackjacks	—More Blackjacks
—Most player losses by Stiffs left standing, or with Standing Hands one or two points lower than Dlr.	—Most player losses by busting or losses of Standing Hands by two or more points.

cards have been dealt out; by the time that 50% of the cards have been dealt out, it will develop a bias about two-thirds of the time. It's important to remember that these mathematicians, to whom we're indebted for their early research into the game, always held the assumption that they were often in the presence of that rare beast, the Random Deck!

In today's American casinos, the Defensive Deck is what you'll much more likely run into. This means that you could easily be dealing with a deck that develops a bias as soon as the first cards have been dealt out.

Random decks do appear, either fleetingly as a new deck starts to get some use, or, more likely, in an occasional, well-used, well-shuffled deck. Don't ignore its existence, for playing a balanced deck with a biased strategy can easily backfire.

Further on in the book I'll teach you an easy method for tracking the Core cards, so you'll be able to determine what the density of a particular Core is, but first I'd like to describe the two types of games that evolve, one with a Heavy (or Dense) Core, the other with a Light (or Hollow) Core.

THE INFLUENCE OF THE HEAVY CORE

There are sixteen Core cards in every fifty-two card deck. That's four per thirteen, or roughly 31% of the deck. A two-deck game would have thirty-two Core cards; an eight-deck shoe would have eight times sixteen, or 128 Core cards. There are also sixteen tens per deck, but the sixteen Core cards have more influence on the game than the sixteen tens do.

Let's say that we're in a two-deck game, with four players at the table. The first hand is dealt out, the Dealer shows a four, so only a couple people take hits. About a quarter of one deck has been used up, twelve or thirteen cards, but you've noticed that only one of those cards was a Core card—say, a seven. So, after that first hand you would describe the Core of the deck as being heavier, since it has more 5–8s than a normal deck of that size would have. What would be the influence on the game with a remaining deck that's developed an excess of Core cards?

You will notice the game starting to get calmer, more laborious. Because of extra 5–8s more fifteens, sixteens, seventeens, and eighteens will start to appear. Breaking activity goes down, because people don't choose to hit those hands very often. Those fortunate enough to get a twelve, thirteen or fourteen will take more successful hits—that is, unless the dealer shows a 2–7, which will cause many of them to stand. If the dealer turns over a twelve, thirteen or fourteen, she will probably hit successfully because 5–8 combine so well with those stiffs; dealer busting will be less overall, in any case.

More double down opportunities will appear, perhaps cheering up some players, until they take the poor hit that they're more likely to receive with a Heavy Core. Fewer blackjacks will be dealt, in fact, fewer decent hands altogether—nineteens, twenties, or blackjacks. The general trends of the game will be a lot of inferior hands for the players (mostly 15–18) against a lot of standing hands for the dealer.

The dealer will often beat by one point those who happen to get a standing hand. That's because 11 of 20 hits by Core cards taken on stiffs add up to 19 or more. Many player losses will be by those left holding stiffs while praying for a dealer bust. Those players assuming that the dealer's down card is always a Ten will find that they're wrong most of the time, or that, even when they're right, the dealer still ends up taking effective hits.

A recap: A slow game with general hand range 15 thru 18, with more double downs, which take more lousy hits. A lot of stiffs left standing and losing whenever the dealer shows two thru seven, for the dealer will take more effective hits than usual. Few blackjacks. Less breaking activity.

Combine this Heavy Core with certain casino defenses and the game becomes even more predictable. The two casino defenses again: 1) clumps of high cards followed by clumps of low cards; 2) the high/low/high/low order.

How do you, as a Core Player, react to this Heavy Core?

First of all, the Heavy Core is the least advantageous type of deck to play with. So keep the betting conservative. If you're lucky enough to get a twelve, thirteen or fourteen, your chances of hitting and markedly improving your hand are better. A look at Table #3 shows that, with only one exception, Core cards combine with twelve, thirteen and fourteen to make standing hands.

So what if tens will bust the Dealer's stiffs? You'll have to play your stiffs (hard 12–16) first. More than one-third of your two card hands will be hard stiffs. And you'll have to play them before you even know if the dealer has one.

Tracking tens is just a shadow game. As you see here, if you take a ten, it will bust your stiff; if you don't, you still have the stiff.

By utilizing a "Completion Principle," the Core cards let you play hard twelve through sixteen more aggressively. Seventy percent of the Core card/stiff combinations make standing hands (fourteen of twenty).

TABLE #3

Third Card

		2	3	4	5	6	7	8	9	10	10	10	10	A
	9	11	12	13	14	15	16	17	18	19	19	19	19	10/20
	10	12	13	14	15	16	17	18	19	20	20	20	20	21
	11	13	14	15	16	17	18	19	20	21	21	21	21	12
Two Card Hand Total	12	14	15	16	17	18	19	20	21	B	B	B	B	13
	13	15	16	17	18	19	20	21	B	B	B	B	B	14
	14	16	17	18	19	20	21	B	B	B	B	B	B	15
	15	17	18	19	20	21	B	B	B	B	B	B	B	16
	16	18	19	20	21	B	B	B	B	B	B	B	B	17

So what if tens will bust the dealer's stiffs? You'll have to play your stiffs (hard 12-16) first. More than one-third of your two card hands will be hard stiffs. And you'll have to play them before you even know if the dealer has one.

Tracking tens is just a shadow game. As you see here, if you take a ten, it will bust your stiff; if you don't, you still have the stiff.

By utilizing a "Completion Principle," the Core cards let you play hard 1 through 16 more aggressively. Seventy percent of the Core card/stiff combinations make standing hands (14 of 20). None leave you with a stiff. Over half make a total of nineteen or more (11 of 20). Only hands of nineteen or more give you a favorable chance to beat the dealer. You will lose the majority of hands that total eighteen or less.

A Heavy Core improves your hits on stiffs. Hard Doubles, as the Table shows, should be avoided with the Heavy Core.

None leave you with a stiff. Over half make a total of nineteen or more (eleven of twenty). Only hands of nineteen or more give you a favorable chance to beat the dealer. You will lose the majority of hands that total eighteen or less.

A Heavy Core improves your hits on stiffs. Hard doubles, as Table #3 shows, should be avoided with the Heavy Core. Of course, if you suspect that you're in the middle of a clump of tens, then your options are cut considerably. You must either stand with your stiff and hope the dealer turns over a stiff *and* hits it with one of those tens, or hope that the clump has ended, or that you'll just get lucky and take a good hit. When I know that the deck's in the midst of a high clump, I usually don't take a hit if a ten will bust me.

When playing with a Heavy Core, if you get dealt a nine, ten or eleven, resist the impulse to double down. Even if you believe that the deck's into a clump of high cards, I would still resist the temptation. With a Heavy Core, it's just not worth it.

With the Heavy Core, don't make the assumption that the dealer's down card is always ten. This is a bad way to play at any time. After all, only 31% of the deck are tens. Of course, if you believe that you're in a strong clump of tens, it's another matter.

There is less breaking activity with a Heavy Core. You'll find that when the dealer is showing two to six, she'll usually make her hand with a Heavy Core. Unless you think you're in the midst of a clump of tens, you should hit your twelve or thirteen to attempt a standing hand. What?! you may exclaim. Hit a twelve or thirteen against a dealer's five or six? Never!

While I agree that this is a sensational development in the world of Basic Strategy, I assure you that I'll provide firm mathematical proof for all the new strategies that I propose. When Dr. Thorp first proposed to an uninformed public that they'd do better hitting their sixteens vs. Dealer's ten, he was met with a chorus of hoots. Today it is widely accepted that, "given a random deck," a player has a 23.4% chance of winning hitting sixteen against a ten showing, compared to a 22.8% chance of winning if he stands—a gain of .6 hands per 100. Thorp also knew that with each ten gone from the remaining deck, his chances of winning sixteen vs. Dlr. ten increased about 1%, that each extra ten in the remaining deck decreased his chances by the 1%.

His knowledge of the effects of depletion or addition of tens for each particular situation was what made his Ten Tracking System so powerful for him. Basic Strategy wasn't enough—he had to change things as the deck developed depletions or excesses.

The CORE System uses the same principle. Consider these brief tables:

Normal % of Player Disadvantage when Hitting vs. Stndg.	VS.	5	6 (Stnd. on Soft 17)		
		Dealer's Up Card			
12		−2%	−.75%		
13		−8%	−7%		

% Advantage Increase w/each extra Core card in deck when hitting with extra:	VS.	5	6	7	8
		Dealer 5			
12		+1.2%	+1.3%	+.9%	+1.3%
13		+2%	+2%	+1.4%	+1.6%
	VS.	Dealer 6			
12		+1.1%	+.7%	+.9%	+1.4%
13		+1.9%	+1.2%	+1.4	+1.6%

What these charts are saying is, starting from the top, that Player's twelve is normally 2% better off standing than hitting against Dealer five. With a balanced deck you will average losses 58% of the times that you stand in this situation, and losses 60% of the times you hit, a difference of 2%. The Player twelve vs. Dealer six figures are stand: lose 58%, hit: lose 59%, a difference of about 1%—actually .75%. However, if the (single) remaining deck has two extra Core cards in it, say, a five and a seven, the chances of winning when hitting Player twelve vs. Dealer five improve 2.1% = +.1% improvement, the two extra Core cards making it slightly more advantageous to hit your twelve vs. Dealer Five. If you're holding twelve vs Dealer Six, it takes only two extra Core cards to make it advantageous to hit your twelve vs. Dealer Six.

It's not too difficult to figure out the logic behind these moves. A brief look at Table #3 shows that the 5–8 Core cards are just the thing to combine with twelve and thirteen. All eight totals are standing hands, five of them nineteen or above. And when you have the knowledge that the deck contains a Heavy Core, you can turn your twelves, thirteens, and fourteens (which you'll receive once every four deals) into winning hands! You won't be duped into losing double bets to the house just because you have the opportunity to double down. But, best of all, if you see that the deck is going to continue in the same laborious fashion, you should have the knowledge and forbearance to LEAVE!

THE INFLUENCE OF THE LIGHT CORE

When the deck becomes depleted of Core cards we say that the Core is lighter, or more hollow. If you know what this means you will have a definite advantage over the house.

The trademarks of the Light Core are these: a more active, lively game. More nineteens, twenties and blackjacks will show on initial deals. Double down opportunities won't show as often, but when they do, you have a much better chance of taking a good hit. The number of twelves, thirteens and fourteens will be reduced considerably, the fifteens and sixteens not quite as much, but still a bit. Busting activity goes up for both the players and the dealer. Take this opportunity to put the onus on the dealer: make her make her hand. She *has to* in order for the house to win. You don't.

As the 5–8 Core begins to lighten, you'll stop hitting your twelves and thirteens against Dealer two and three. It soon becomes advantageous to stand with your fifteens and sixteens vs. dealer ten. Overall, hard stiffs will be hit less aggressively by the player.

Aside from the Core values, there are nine other card denominations. Two-thirds of these are high—nines, tens and aces. The other third are twos, threes and fours. But, if clumping is present, it means that the remainder of the deck might not show any particular bias towards the high end. In other words, a Light Core doesn't automatically mean a high ten count.

When you're into the Light Core, it's a period of strategic advantage, so you can raise your bet at this time. But remember, the chance of busting also goes up. A lot of systems ignore the fact that if the dealer's chance of a bust goes up, so almost always does the player's. Don't forget the terms of the trade-off: You're going to get more nineteens, twenties and blackjacks, and better hits on your double downs, but you must take a bigger chance of busting on your stiffs. Watch the clumps to try to make the dealer bust instead. And don't make your raise *too* large.

Personally, I prefer to play in one and two deck games. I watch for decks that have a clump of high cards at one end and a clump that includes some Core cards at the other end. The one and two deck games also give me a chance to make radical strategy changes as soon as the first cards are dealt out, especially if they happen to be Core cards!

Not only is it faster and easier to recognize clumps in the smaller decks, but a deck that shows a Heavy Core clump on one shuffle has a fair chance of turning over and dealing that Core on the first deal of the next shuffle. This provides a quick chance to raise your bet in the confidence of the Light Core. And the bet raise does not have to be dramatic to produce some dramatic results in the long run.

I find that a simple 50% raise during Light Core periods, flat betting during unbiased periods, and a 50% drop from that flat bet during Heavy Core periods gives me very satisfactory results. This is a betting ratio of just 2:1, or 3:1. It gives me effective bet change mobility and tends to keep little attention coming my way when I do raise and win.

If I happen to lose my smaller, Heavy Core bet and make a raise for the Light Core, it gives me the profile of a "bet chaser," who the casinos usually love. Rarely do I double my bet. There is too much stress on getting in big raises these days.

Ahh—all so much easier said than done....

In succeeding chapters I'll show you the methods that have paid off so well for me. You'll learn ways with which to rapidly read a deck, how to recognize what defenses you're up against in a particular game, see new strategy charts to use during Heavy and Light Core periods, as well as ways of spotting winning tables before you even sit down or look at one card.

If you're presently a Ten Counter, then you'll have the advantage of already knowing how to track portions of a deck. And, if you've never tracked a single card, you're going to be surprised at how easy and effective the whole thing can be. In either case, you are about to learn a strategy that is so far removed from the standard manner of playing Blackjack that dealers and pit bosses *and* players will probably take you for a lucky numbskull before they suspect you of using a system.

Styles of play change, shuffles change, the casinos change and so do the players, but the deck and its mathematics remain the same.

Chapter 4.

Blackjack Is a Fluid Game

(How To Adjust Your Play From The First Cards Dealt)

This is the chapter that demonstrates the mathematical soundness of the CORE System. It's filled with the charts, tables, numbers that some players find so utterly boring, while others see them as fascinating proof that they can become winners.

As I've said before, the best players, at their best moments, are aware of only the probabilities and trends of the game. In order to combine the "frozen moments" presented in these charts with the movement of a blackjack game you must train your senses to *spot the trends.* Some people can do this by merely scanning the following charts. Others will want to study them intently.

Don't confuse "trends" with "streaks" or "hunches." Streaks and hunches are valid things in the world of gambling, and they can even be tied to mathematics, but they are things that are happening "now"—spontaneous opportunities which you might or might not grab in the seconds that they become available. A "trend," as far as this treatise is concerned, is something that has a viable set of signposts, with mathematical basis, or that shows symptoms of strong, reliable mathematical influence. "Trend" is where math merges with experience and intuition. It's a place where charts become functional reality, and where "frozen" becomes "fluid."

Spotting a trend is the best you can hope for in this game. It's my theory that, even if you always knew the dealer's down card, or even the order of every card in the deck, you could still lose! Who's to stop that little old lady who, after seventy years of blackjack abstinence, has decided to pick your table at which to learn the game? Nothing can keep her from hitting her eighteen. The next hand she stubbornly stands on nine. All "advice" she views with suspicion.

I've learned not to become upset with this type of player. Half the time they end up doing something that causes the dealer to lose, anyhow! Their existence is no different than an extra shuffle to the deck. When a winning trend is present and strong, almost nothing will overcome it. Spotting trends, while on one hand is the most you can hope for, is, on the other hand, more than adequate to turn you into a winner. (If you want some proof of how little knowing what the dealer's down card is worth, try playing a game of "Double Exposure" Blackjack, where the dealer's down card is exposed, and notice how many hands you still lose.)

When you play, you face not only a total deck, you face certain situations. Table #4 outlines the situation of facing certain Dealer Up Cards combined with depletions of specific card values from the remaining deck. The top row, from left to right, lists the various Dealer Up Cards, with the average percentage for dealer bust showing right under each Up Card. The left column shows the card values that may have already been dealt from the deck. For instance: If the Dealer Up Card is five (42.9% dealer bust probability), and you know that a six

TABLE #4†

Dealer Shows:	2	3	4	5	6	7	8	9	T*	A*	Average Absolute Effect ↓
Dlr. Bust %:	35.3	37.6	40.1	42.9	42.1	26.0	23.9	23.3	21.4	11.7	
2	.1	.1	.1	.8	.8	.2	.2	.2	-.3	0.0	.285
3	.1	.1	.8	.9	.9	.3	.3	-.2	-.3	0.0	.369
4	.2	.8	.9	1.0	1.0	.4	-.1	-.2	-.3	.1	.454
5	.9	1.0	1.1	1.1	1.1	0.0	-.1	-.2	-.2	.2	.500
6	.8	.8	.9	.9	-.1	-.2	-.3	-.4	-.5	1.0	.569
7	.6	.7	.7	-.3	-.3	-.5	-.5	-.6	.6	.7	.562
8	.4	.5	-.5	-.5	-.5	-.6	-.7	.4	.4	.4	.469
9	.2	-.7	-.7	-.7	-.7	-.9	.3	.2	.2	.1	.408
T	-.9	-.9	-.9	-.9	-.9	.1	.1	.1	.1	-.6	.446
A	.5	.4	.4	.3	1.3	.7	.6	.5	.1	-.1	.400

Gone From Deck: (rows 2 through A)

}.525 (bracketing rows 5 through 8)

*Bust % when you don't know
if the dealer has blackjack.

Average of 5–8 Core [.525] – t [.446] = [.079]

[.079] [.446] = .177, meaning that the 5–8 Cord cards are 17.7% more influential to change in dealer bust probability then are tens.

is gone from the remaining deck, you would add .9 to the normal dealer bust probability. 42.9% + .9% = 43.8% chance of dealer bust with that six gone from the deck.

If the number on the chart is a negative number (e.g. –.5), you would *subtract* that amount from dealer's bust probability. And, if you changed all of the negative numbers to positives, and all of the positives to negatives (excepting the Dealer Bust Probability and the Average

†This chart contains some material (scaled down from hundreths to tenths) taken from Peter Griffin's *Theory Of Blackjack*, Edward Thorp's *Beat The Dealer*, as well as some of my own material.

Absolute Effect figures on the far right), you would have an accurate chart of how Surplus Card Values affect dealer bust probability. Both views are equally valid. I've chosen to show card values already dealt because we see cards leaving the remaining deck as we play, and it's easier, initially, to think in that direction. Needless to say, surpluses are usually created in some other card values at the same time.

However, positive or negative is not really the question. The most advantageous thing to do is to track the cards that effect the most overall change, be it positive or negative. Change is an absolute value, relative to what came before it. It doesn't matter whether it goes over, under, up, down or inside out, it's still change. Therefore, in the columns on the far right, I've calculated what I call the Average Absolute Effect for each of the possible depleted card values. This is the sum of each line of figures from left to right, ignoring their positive or negative signs (this is called an absolute number), and dividing by thirteen (the number of possible Dealer Up Cards. There are four cards worth ten, making thirteen.). I've taken these averages out to three decimal places to make it easier to view their differences.

It's not surprising that the two and three, the lowest valued cards, are the least influential in terms of Absolute Effect on dealer bust probability. What's surprising is that they're directly followed by ace, nine and ten as the least influential cards. It's not the large valued cards that make the most difference—do you see how the four does more than the nine? It's the medium range cards, the Core cards, that show the biggest effect in this chart.

The actual order, from greatest to least influence on dealer's bust probability, is:

Six	=	.569
Seven	=	.562
Five	=	.500
Eight	=	.469
Four	=	.454
Ten	=	.446
Nine	=	.408
Ace	=	.400
Three	=	.369
Two	=	.285

.525

.525 [avg. CORE Effect]
−.446 [Ten effect]
.079 = 17.7% of .446 [Ten effect]
Meaning that surpluses or
depletions of CORE cards effect
17.7% more overall change than do
Tens on Dealer Bust Probability.

But is it really that surprising that the 5–8 Core cards effect the most change? After all, a wheel revolves around its center, not the other way around. And blackjack card values revolve around their center, or the 5–8 Core cards.

It's not necessary to memorize this chart to become a better player. I don't have it memorized and I win at four of every five sittings. What would be more helpful to you would be to study the chart for patterns. You don't even have to understand the implications of the patterns that you might spot. The point is to spot them. And from there, your mind will soon learn to spot trends. Once you see a trend, it's not a very big jump to be able to judge if it's a bad or good trend. Why? Because "trend" is where math overlaps with experience and intuition.

But let's get back to the mathematics, lest you get the misimpression that I'm teaching you a giant guessing game. I'm not. The CORE System is absolutely, mathematically sound.

Table #5 is a good chart to start with because you're going to face this situation (hard stiffs twelve thru sixteen vs. Dealer ten) about once in every 8.8 hands (11.34% of the time).

This chart shows the effects of depletion from the

TABLE #5*

11.34% of hands

Hard Stiffs vs. Dlr. Ten [1 of every 8.8 hands]

Hand Total:	12	13	14	15	16	AAE		1.44 − 1.28 = .16 (12½%)
Gain of Hit Over Stand:	14%	11%	7%	3%	1%			
5	.2	−.3	−.8	−1.8	−2.6	1.14		
6	0.0	−.4	−1.4	−2.2	1.6	1.12	1.44	
7	−2.1	−3.2	−4.2	−.5	−.7	2.14		
8	−2.9	−3.5	.2	.1	−.1	1.36		
T	1.4	1.4	1.3	1.2	1.1	1.28		
A	.1	0.0	−.1	−.2	−.5	.2		

(left label: "Gone From Deck:" beside rows 5, 6, 7, 8, T, A)

In this common situation, the absence or surplus (in the remaining deck) of (5–8) Core cards [1.44] has 12½% more influence than do tens [1.28] on changing your hitting advantage.

remaining deck of the card values listed on the left, when the dealer is holding a ten, and you hold the hands twelve thru sixteen, listed along the top. The numbers directly under the Player's Hand Totals show the advantage (or, when a negative number, the disadvantage) realized when *hitting* that hand against the Dealer's ten.

For example: If you have a fifteen against a Dealer's ten, and you know that a five is gone from the remaining deck, your advantage for that play decreases − 1.8%. Deduct 1.8% from the normal advantage of 3% and you have + 1.2% remaining. This tells you that you still have a 1.2% advantage hitting your hard fifteen against Dealer's ten. With one five gone from the deck, you will still win 1.2 more hands than you lose when you hit

*This chart contains some material (scaled down from hundreths to tenths) taken from Peter Griffin's *Theory Of Blackjack*, Edward Thorp's *Beat The Dealer*, as well as some of my own material.

facing this exact situation 100 times. When the remainder of this calculation becomes a negative number,
it means that your advantage has turned to disadvantage,
in other words, that hitting is no longer the best move.

Again, give attention to the Average Absolute Effects
listed on the right side of the chart. The average change
effected by the Core cards in this ticklish but common
situation is 1.44%. For every extra and/or missing ten in
the remaining deck, the effect is only 1.28%. The
difference of these two values $(1.44 - 1.28 = .16)$
shows that the Core cards have 12.5% more influence in
this situation than tens do. $(.16 = 12.5\%$ of $1.28)$ The
ace's influence of .2 is hardly worth mentioning.

Okay! Now what, you may ask, am I doing? On one
hand I'm saying that math specifics aren't that important,
then, with my next breath, I inundate you with moun-
tains of microscopic figures!

Well, just hang on a little longer, because what you
have just learned (the Principle of Card Depletions and
Surpluses) will be the basis of the first improvement in
your play. Now you're going to see how to apply it to the
Fringe Plays of blackjack. What are the Fringe Plays?

Fringe Plays are what I have named the most exasperating situations that we players have to deal with:

> twelve vs. Dealer two and three
> thirteen vs. Dealer two and three
> sixteen vs. Dealer ten
> Twelve!

Doubling eleven vs. Dealer ace
Doubling nine vs. Dealer two and three
Soft Doubling A,6 + A,7 vs. Dealer two and three

Though all of the above may not ring a bell with you,
I'm sure that anyone with a little experience in the game

has felt the inner battle of Impulse vs. Fear that at least some of these situations can produce in a player. These are among the hardest choices that chance throws at blackjack players. And, somehow, even if the player claims to ignore math, his body responds with exasperation when encountering these "borderline" choices.

By a happy coincidence, it's these very plays that are the first to be affected by surpluses or deficits in the Core! This means that you can adjust your decisions for these plays from the very first cards that come out of the deck. These are the plays that are on the edge of change. This is why I call them the Fringe Plays. The moves that Basic Strategy dictates for these plays are so easily influenced by the deficits or surpluses of one or two Core cards that when facing them, you can quickly improve your chances if you know how.

Take a look at Table #6. The center chart shows traditional moves for playing your twelves and thirteens vs. Dealer two thru six *given a random deck.* Well, we already know that the Random Deck is an endangered species. But, even if you happen to find one, Table #6 shows us how readily an imbalance of one or two cards can change your chances playing these two hands. *When you are dealt a hard stiff you're already at a disadvantage, because you're going to lose most of those hands. You can passively accept this, either by helplessly watching the dealer make her hand, or blindly, impulsively hitting, maybe busting out. Or, you can aggressively go on the attack, and win more of those hands!*

Of the ten situations presented here (Hard twelve and thirteen vs. Dealer two thru six), the CORE System is offering you a way to aggressively respond, at least some

TABLE #6

HITTING HARD 12 & 13 vs. Dlr. 2 Thru 6

When
Hitting:

Dlr. Up Card					
	2	3	4	5	6
13	S	S	S	S	S
12	-3	-2	S	S	S

LIGHT CORE
(Deficit of 5–8
per remaining deck)

Dlr. Up Card					
	2	3	4	5	6
13	S	S	S	S	S
12	H	H	S	S	S

NORMAL DECK
(Thorp & Braun's
Basic Strategy)

Dlr. Up Card					
	2	3	4	5	6
13	+1	+2	+4	+6	+6
12	H	H	+1	+2	+2

HEAVY CORE
(Surplus 5–8 per
remaining deck

Numbers indicate what Core Count changes Basic Strategy.

What these charts are saying is this: If you are holding hard thirteen and you are facing a Dealer two, Traditional Basic Strategy calls for you to stand and hope for a dealer bust, which will happen in a normal deck about 35% of the time. You lose the other 65%. But, if you know that this is just one extra Core card in the remaining deck, you can take a hit with the confidence that your 35% chance of winning is increased. Any Core card will combine with thirteen to make a standing hand, putting more pressure on the dealer. The secret is this: Make sure that you're not in a solid clump of tens.

of the time, to all ten. In six of those ten situations you will notice that it takes merely *one or two* Core cards, either way, to let you improve your chances.

Except for twenty (dealt Player 10.6% of the time), you will receive hard twelve and thirteen more than any other hands (16.7% of the time—one of every six hands.) Twenty plays itself. The better you handle twelve and thirteen, the better player you will be.

For now, let me explain a simple logic—so simple that it seems to have missed a lot of players.

If you add the values of the Core cards (five thru

eight) to the hard hands (twelve and thirteen), you will, in every case come up with a standing hand.

12 becomes 17, 18, 19 or 20.
13 becomes 18, 19, 20 or 21.

The reason the CORE System is so effective for your Hard Stiffs (twelve thru sixteen) is that, in fourteen out of twenty cases (70% of the time) the Core cards combine to make a standing hand (See Table #3). At no time will they leave you with a stiff. I call it "The Completion Principle."

You are no longer at the mercy of waiting for the dealer to bust, if you remain aware of how light or heavy the Core is. (A simple way of tracking the Core will be shown in Chapter 5.) No longer are you at the mercy of the massive card clumps with which the casinos defend themselves, because the CORE System tracks only four card values.* The Core cards are a clump in their own right! It is not unusual to find at least two of the Core values in a casino card clump. We have seen how influential the absence or addition of a couple Core cards can be in the Fringe Plays. (Charts for the additional Fringe Plays follow in this chapter.)

The casinos already clump tens. They clump aces. They clump small cards. If they start clumping or separating the fives, sixes, sevens and eights, they might

---

*Even one of the most advanced counting systems in use today, "Hi-Opt," demands that you track at least eight card values, four of which are tens. Most systems track more cards. This makes them helpless against casino clumping. And clumping is why casino blackjack profits are now higher than they have ever been.

as well just start stacking the deck, and then we'll really cash in!

The charts that follow in this chapter will be similar to Table #6, in that they will show you simple strategy charts of the Fringe Plays listed in the first part of this chapter. By using these charts you will, during a Fringe Play, be able to adjust your response from the first cards dealt out of the deck. Mastery of this concept will allow you to aggressively combat, with more skill, the most frustrating, exasperating (and, often, most common) hands of the game.

Complete strategy charts are provided in the Appendices at the back of the book.

TIP: TRAIN YOURSELF TO REMEMBER THE FIRST TWO
CORE CARDS THAT APPEAR.

This is a good mental exercise for sharpening your attention. It also allows you to make more specific changes in strategy as soon as the first cards have been dealt. (For games of four decks or less.)

As a quick example, look back again at Table #5. If you were playing a single deck game and you received a nine and a six for a fifteen vs. Dealer ten, and you happened to see a five in your neighbor's hand, you could make a note that the first two Core cards that you saw were five and six. Normal Strategy tells you to hit your fifteen vs. Dealer ten, with a 3% advantage over standing. Knowing that a five and six are already depleted from the deck tells you that -4% has been depleted from your hitting advantage. Three $-$ four $= -1\%$, or a disadvantage of 1% if you hit your fifteen vs. Dealer ten.

Why? With Dealer showing ten, her probabilities of ending up with nineteen, twenty, twenty-one, or blackjack are 55.85%. With a five and six already gone from the deck, two of the eight cards that will make your fifteen (9,6) into a twenty or twenty-one are already used up early in the deck; your chances are being seriously affected in terms of hitting. And, if you know, early on, that there are extras of these cards, your chances are favorably increased.

The Completion Principle is aptly illustrated in Table #3. It also shows that when you are tracking tens, you are merely playing a shadow game in regard to your stiffs. Those stiffs make up 36.8% of all two-card hands—more than one of every three. What will a ten do for a stiff? If you take it, you bust. If you don't, you still have the stiff. This built-in application of The Completion Principle by the CORE System is one of the main reasons it's so effective.

SOME COMPARISONS BETWEEN THE TRADITIONAL BLACKJACK PLAYER AND THE CORE PLAYER

TRADITIONAL BASIC STRATEGIST/ TEN TRACKER/AVERAGE PLAYER	THE CORE PLAYER
1) The main object of play is to get high hands.	1) High hands play themselves. The main object is to play stiffs and lower hands well. They make up most of the game.
2) Tens and aces are the highest, and therefore, the most important cards. The game turns around them.	2) The game turns around the middle range, Core cards, just as a wheel turns around its center.

3) A lot of tens will cause the dealer's busting rate to go up.

3) When dealer busting goes up, so, almost always, does player busting. And too many tens just make many hands of twenty, causing pushes with the dealer.

4) High and low ten counts tell me when the deck is rich or poor.

4) Tens comprise barely 31% of the deck. There are nine other card values that also make the deck rich or poor.

5) The deck was at "ideal" ten density (41%). I can't understand why the dealer didn't bust more.

5) Average dealer bust probability is 28.36%. During "ideal" Ten density, that bust probability only rises to about $29\frac{1}{2}$%. I can't sit around praying for dealer busts. I win my hands playing the Core strategies.

6) I use traditional Basic Strategy to have the best mathematical chance to win in each situation. How can a billion computer-played hands be wrong?

6) That old Basic Strategy is fine for a random, or balanced deck. Unfortunately, most decks aren't balanced. All the casino does to ruin Basic Strategy is clump up some cards or put them in a high/low order.

7) I'm tired of losing big bets with high ten counts, then having small bets out on negative Ten counts, as a winning streak goes by. This game is just too much luck!

7) Card clumping has made ten counting useless. I bet according to how Heavy or Light the Core gets. It's the Core, not luck, that makes the game run!

8) You're right. Clumping has made card counting useless. I get inflated, meaningless counts because of clumps. I

8) I track only four card values, an amount less susceptible to clump distortions. And the casino

might as well go back to playing hunches.	makes things predictable by forming clumps. Sometimes, they clump my Core cards for me.
9) The dealer just kept hitting her stiffs for twenty and twenty-one. I couldn't believe her luck!	9) The deck had a Heavy Core, so I kept hitting my stiffs for great hands. Sometimes I even took the dealer's card!

TABLE #7

Hitting 14, 15 & 16 vs. Dlr. Ten

	T
16	-1
15	-2
14	-2

[Stand when 1st Core card is Five]
[Stand when 1st two Core cards are Fives and/or Sixes]
[Stand when 1st two Core cards are Sevens]

Light Core

	T
16	H
15	H
14	H

Normal Deck
(Basic Strategy)

[Stand when Fives are only Core cards dealt]

	T
16	H
15	H
14	H

Heavy Core

Numbers indicate Core Count that changes
Basic Strategy from hitting to standing.

"For playing 16 v. T, the remarkably elementary direction "Stand when there are more sixes than fives remaining, hit otherwise,' is more than 60% efficient."

—Griffin, *Theory of Blackjack*, p. 59

TABLE #8

Doubling 11 vs. Dlr. A, 10 vs. Dlr. T, 9 vs. Dlr. 2 & 3

Light Core

	2	3		T	A
11					-1
10				-2	
9	-1	D			

Normal Deck
(Basic Strategy)

	2	3		T	A
11					H*
10				H	
9	H	D			

*Dbl. when Dlr. hits soft 17

Heavy Core

	2	3		T	A
11					+1
10				H	
9	H	+2			

Numbers indicate Core Count that changes
Basic Strategy from hitting to doubling, or doubling to hitting.

TABLE #9

Doubling A,6 & A,7 vs. Dlr. 2 & 3

Light Core

	2	3
A,7	-1	D
A,6	-1	D

Normal Deck

	2	3
A,7	H	D
A,6	H	H

[Stand at +2]

Heavy Core

	2	3
A,7	S	+2
A,6	H	+2

Numbers indicate Core Counts at which
to double down [except for A,7 vs. Dlr. 3].

The Fringe Plays illustrated in Tables #6–#9 represent about
15.3 of all two card hands that you'll be dealt (about one out of
every 6½).

Chapter 5.

Tracking the Core Ratio

You now know enough about the "whys" and "becauses" of the CORE System. Now you can learn how to track when and if there are deficits or surpluses of Core cards in the remaining deck.

Surplus = Heavy Core, a strategic disadvantage.

Deficit = Light Core, a strategic advantage.

Almost all blackjack systems that have been released prior to the CORE System have depended on some variance of Dr. Edward Thorp's Plus/Minus Counting System. They assign a variety of values to many denominations of the deck, which cancel each other out, making the total deck add up to zero. These systems are subject to defeat by the casino's Defensive Decks, which, as you know, use card clumping to easily distort the counts.

Therefore, the CORE System has discarded two of the major facets of the old tracking methods: 1) We now track only four card values, making the system far less vulnerable to clumping. 2) We are no longer concerned with having a count that makes a deck add up to zero. We will use a "ratio" rather than a count. (A count *is* a sort of ratio, but our Core Ratio is not a count, at least, not in the normal, Plus/Minus sense of the word.)

The method for tracking the Core Ratio is very easy. Even a poor mathematician should have little trouble with it, after a bit of practice. But first let me make some comments about just how precise a player really has to be.

The most common complaint about blackjack systems is that, in order to become a consistent winner, one must turn oneself into a virtual computer. And I feel that this would be a valid complaint, *if it were true.*

I have taken a number of professionally-taught black-jack courses. I have read dozens of books on the topic. It's true that many were chock-full of long tables, tiny, exact numbers and rules that claim to be mathematically efficient, except for places that don't hit soft seventeen and only allow doubling nines on rainy Wednesdays. If you're like me and enjoy working with numbers, then it's not so bad. But, if you're like most people, you don't gain enjoyment by memorizing and adhering to tables of figures that read like life insurance premium scales, demand fanatical discipline and then tell you to enjoy the game.

Becoming a winner at blackjack really doesn't need to be this stringent. In the classes I've taken, one of the most common trains of thought that I ran into was that the successful players, amateur and pro alike, have said that they learned and followed faithfully all the counts and right moves, but that it took the enjoyment out of the game for them. And, most importantly, they said that their game was virtually as good when they just kept *informal counts.* These advanced Ten Counters told me, and each other, that they really didn't do that much math in their heads—they just kept informal track of when the deck was rich or poor in Tens, or they just looked for the signposts of a good game (Chapter 11 will tell you how to do this) and, if they ended up losing a few hands, they just left the table and carried on, since they knew that they'd be successful in the long run.

In other words, they simply learned to spot *successful trends*!

This doesn't mean that you can take all the math out of the game. After all, the game is called "Twenty-One"! It's not called Red-and-Black, Even-or-Odd, or High/Low. The object of the game is to get a higher hand than the dealer, without going over the total of twenty-one. So, unless you break out into a rash when doing addition or subtraction, you'll probably find that you can do a little math and still thoroughly enjoy the game. How far you want to take the math is entirely up to you. And, just like a baseball player or a writer, the more that you learn about your game, the better you'll be at it. Some people just have inborn talents for their game. You might discover talents that you didn't even know you have!

Blackjack does respond well to a disciplined approach, but playing can peck away at your discipline in the most seductive manner. You might break from discipline once and do better than usual. Then, when you try the same thing again, you get hammered. So you return to your program and—lo and behold—you get beaten again!

A disciplined program can help, but you should be careful not to let it keep you from playing a fluid, loose game. Remember:

RELAXED VIGILANCE!

I want to give this concept some rhyme and reason for you, or you may find that forming a playing style to accommodate it can become very expensive. So, we're going to take some time and learn how to track what I call the Core Ratio.

How many Core cards are in a deck? There are sixteen per deck, the same amount as there are tens.* There are thirty-two in a two-deck game; 128 in an eight-deck shoe. This means that there are four Core cards per quarter deck. The *quarter deck* is the unit that we'll use to determine the Core Ratio. (In the CORE System, you could say that each deck adds up to +16, but this isn't very simple.)

CONVERSION CHART FOR CORE CARDS PER QUARTER DECK

	1/4 = 4	(Number of Core cards)
	2/4 = 8	
	3/4 = 12	
one deck	4/4 = 16	
	5/4 = 20	
	6/4 = 24	
	7/4 = 28	
two decks	8/4 = 32	
	9/4 = 36	
	10/4 = 40	
	11/4 = 44	
three decks	12/4 = 48	
	13/4 = 52	
	14/4 = 56	
	15/4 = 60	
four decks	16/4 = 64	
	17/4 = 68	

---

*Those of you who can already track tens will find that combining an informal ten awareness with tracking the Core cards will make a very potent system! Keep this in mind: A ten-rich deck with a Heavy Core is a player-killing game. It's the weight of the Core that determines whether a ten-rich game is really good or not.

$$18/4 = 72$$
$$19/4 = 76$$
five decks $20/4 = 80$ (Each deck = +16)
$$21/4 = 84$$
$$22/4 = 88$$
$$23/4 = 92$$
six decks $24/4 = 96$
$$25/4 = 100$$
$$26/4 = 104$$
$$27/4 = 108$$
seven decks $28/4 = 112$
$$29/4 = 116$$
$$30/4 = 120$$
$$31/4 = 124$$
eight decks $32/4 = 128$

Rarely does an eight-deck shoe get dealt out past six-and-a-half decks, so you usually won't have to go past that, if you're playing shoes.

A simple principle comes into play when you think of the decks or shoes in terms of quarters. Simply multiply the numerator by the denominator (the first number by the second) in the fraction representing the amount of quarter decks and it quickly gives you the number of Core cards that should normally be in a deck that size.

Example: 1-1/2 decks = 6/4 decks. By multiplying 6 × 4 = 24, we know that there are normally twenty-four Core cards in one and a half decks. If one and a half (6/4) decks have been used and you've seen less than twenty-four Core cards dealt out, the remaining deck(s) contain a Heavy Core; if you've seen more than twenty-four, the remaining deck(s) contain a Light Core.

It is a good policy to know how many decks, and therefore how many Core cards are in the game before you start to play. Here is the process again:

—Multiplying the number of decks in the game by four will tell you how many quarter decks that you have.

—Multiplying the numerator by the denominator in the quarter decks number will tell you how many Core cards are in them.

—Learn to count from zero to 128 by fours. (It's on the Conversion Chart.)

The next step is to learn how many quarter decks are in any pile of cards that you're looking at. This is an eyeball job, yet that can be quite effective.

Start with two decks. See what they look like. Remove one and see what it looks like. Put them back together and remove a half deck and see what one and a half decks look like. Casinos that offer hand-held one- and two-deck games often instruct their dealers to hold the decks tightly and slide the top cards forward. You can learn to read the amount of quarter decks even though they are tilted like that. Or you can do what I do, which is to simply look at the discard pile, usually kept stacked to the side in normal fashion, and add the cards on the table for the current hand to the number in the used pile.

For estimating the amounts remaining in four-, six- and eight-deck shoes, you will have to learn to approximate the number of quarter decks while the cards have that peculiar slant that they get in a shoe. Sometimes part of the shoe covers the front section of the cards, so you can't see them all. It's not hard to learn to assign a value to that unseen part, because its size never changes. Try doing it while the shoe is completely full, before the first cards are dealt out. During the game, if the casino keeps the discards visible, directly in the back of the shoe, or piled to the side on the table, this can make your mid-game estimations that much easier.

A person who plays only single-deck games isn't going to have a hard job keeping track of the Core count. But single- and double-deck games are difficult, if not impossible, to find in Atlantic City. And some people prefer playing shoes, because they like the chances for streaks and higher betting sequences that shoes can offer. These players must learn the concept of the Real Ratio.

A ratio is a relation in quantity between two things of different sizes.

If Player A loses $500 out of a $1,000 stake, while Player B loses $5 out of a $10 stake, they have both lost half of their money. Player A has lost considerably more than Player B, but it should be clear that, in terms of ratios, they'll each feel like, and, in fact, truly have each lost half of their money. Player A simply had to lose more money to feel that way, because he had a bigger stake to start with.

By the same token, it should be clear to you that one deck with four Core cards missing from it isn't going to act the same as *eight* decks with four Core cards missing from them. An eight-deck shoe will have to lose thirty-two Core cards to act like one deck that's lost four. Therefore, to make accurate use of the Core strategy charts (which are devised for one deck), you must, in games with more than one deck, learn to calculate the Real Ratio when the Core becomes lighter or heavier.

I think it'd be more practical if I showed how to do this through four examples. These will show real situations encountered in the one-deck, two-deck, four-deck and eight-deck games. So read all four examples, even if you don't play or enjoy all four types of games:

The Real Ratio

Example #1: One-Deck Game

One deck = 4/4 4 × 4 = 16 Core cards in one deck.

If half the deck has been dealt out, and you've already seen twelve Core cards, you know that the remaining half deck has a Light Core. Why? Because there are sixteen Core cards in one whole deck, and you've already seen twelve dealt out with the first half, leaving only four in the remaining half.

1/2 deck = 2/4 2 × 4 = 8 Core cards normally in 1/2 deck

4 (Core cards actually left) minus 8 (Core cards normally left) = −4

−4 ÷ 2/4 = −8 (a Real Ratio of −8, a *very* Light Core)

Why? Because a half deck missing four Core cards will act the same as a whole deck missing eight. The Real Ratio is a light Core of −8 (a time of strategic advantage).

The mathematical process here is simple: 1) Multiply the number of surplus Core cards (a [+] number) or deficit Core cards (a minus number) by four (the denominator in the number of quarter decks, always four)*, and 2) Divide the product of that number by the number of quarter decks remaining (the numerator in the number of quarter decks).

Using the above example once again:

−4 (Core deficit) times 4 (always times 4, since we deal in quarter decks) = − 16.

---

*When multiplying and/or dividing positive (+) and negative (−) numbers, remember these rules:

(+) by (+) = (+)

(+) by (−) = (−)

(−) by (−) = (+)

-16 divided by 2 (number of quarter decks in 1/2 deck) $= -8$ (the Real Ratio).

Real Ratios of plus/minus five or greater call for extreme strategy changes. The smaller the total deck, the more likely that you'll encounter larger imbalances in the Core, especially with clumping what it is today. In the above case, we have a very Light Core (-8). It's a good time to raise your bet. Two-card hands that are constructed of cards five thru eight aren't as likely to occur (see Tables #1 & #2).

If you should happen to be dealt a hard stiff (12–16), you know that there are no more than four Core cards left to combine with them. Some may have just been dealt out in the current hand. You should probably stand with your stiff, even with a Dealer ten. You can double down on your hard doubles more aggressively. Don't double down on most soft doubles (except A,6 and A,7, which benefit by the absence of Core cards.)

Remember: Consider how well or how poorly your hand combines with 5,6,7,8, keeping in mind that, in this example, those cards are not readily available.

Always be aware of clumping, if it's present*
The Real Ratio
Example #2: Two-Deck Game

Two decks = 8/4 8 × 4 = 32 Core cards in a two deck game.

Know how many decks and how many Core cards are in your game before you start to play.

You see 5/4 decks in the discard pile. You've seen only

---

*Chapter seven discusses the types of clumping in the Defensive Deck.

fourteen Core cards. Therefore, you know that the Core
has become Heavy in the remaining deck, because you
should have seen twenty Core cards ($5 \times 4 = 20$).
What is the Real Ratio for the remaining 3/4 deck?

32 (# Core cards in two decks) minus 14 (Core cards
actually seen) = 18

18 minus 12 (3/4 dk. normally has 12 Core cards) =
+6

$+6 \div 3/4 = +8$

The Real Ratio is $+8$, an extremely Heavy Core. In
other words, 3/4 of a deck with six extra Core cards will
act like 4/4 (one) deck with eight extra Core cards. It's a
matter of ratios. (The strategy charts are all based on
calculations for one whole deck.)

When you receive your two-card hand, ask yourself
how it combines with 5,6,7,8. If you get a two-card
12–14 (more likely with a Heavy Core), you know that
you can hit it more aggressively, because twelve, thirteen and fourteen combine well with 5–8. Hard doubles
(also more likely with a Heavy Core) *don't.*

Always be aware of clumping, if it's present.

The Real Ratio.

Example #3: The Four-Deck Shoe

Four decks = $16/4$ $16 \times 4 = 64$ Core cards in four
decks.

You have determined that there are two-and-one-half
undealt decks. Two-and-one-half = $10/4 = 40$ Core
cards.

Sixty-four minus forty (# cards in 10/4 dks.) = 24
Core cards normally seen with 6/4 decks used. You have
counted thirty Core cards already, so you know that the
Core is Light. How Light?

$24 - 30 = -6$ $-6 \div 10/4 \text{ (dks)} = -2.4$

Or: $-6 \div 10$ (from 10/4 dks.) $= -.6$ and
$-.6 \times 4$ (from 10/4 dks) $= -2.4$

Whichever is easier for you.

Now what's so easy about that? Possibly not very much, if you're in the heat of an actual game. If you find it's not so easy, try this:

Informal Count: You know that the remaining two-and-one-half decks are light six Core cards (-6).

You know that $-6 \div 2$ (dks) $= -3$

You know that $-6 \div 3$ (dks) $= -2$

Therefore, you can assume that the answer to $-6 \div$ 2-1/2 dks is a Real Ratio somewhere between -2 and -3. So play your strategies as if you have a good, strong, solid -2 Light Core. (Don't push it and act as if it's -3, because the Light Core is only *between* -2 and -3. Play it safe.) You'll find your play to be effective for every Light Core strategy change within the -2 range. That covers a lot of ground.

As I've mentioned before, I personally always use an informal count. I derive more enjoyment from the game and that helps me play better. I've found that spotting and following the trends in a game gives me good strategic command.

The Real Ratio.

Example #4: The Eight-Deck Shoe

Eight decks $= 32/4$ $32 \times 4 = 128$ Core cards in eight decks.

You've gone through two and a half (10/4) decks and have seen forty Core cards. Ten times four equals forty (The amount of Core cards normally in 10/4 decks.) The Core count is: 0, even, zilch.

Forget what's already been dealt. Start your count over. It will be more accurate, because your shoe is now temporarily smaller. (Just five and a half decks remaining: 5-1/2 = 22/4. 22 × 4 = 88 Core cards left.) This strategy move applies anytime that your Real Ratio becomes "0." It will sharpen your game, because the deck will become smaller, and it will keep the numbers more manageable.

Always be aware of clumping, if it's present.

In the previous four examples, did you notice how, as more decks entered the game, the swings in the Real ratio became smaller? A single or double deck game can easily produce a ratio of ±6 or ±8. But in an eight deck shoe, a Real Ratio of ±3 might involve fifteen, eighteen, twenty or more Core cards. So, if you're playing shoes, don't let a ratio like ±2 fool you. Shoe counts involve more cards, so ±2 can be as serious as in any one- or two-deck game.

The Core is so influential to the game of blackjack that the right moves combined with a ±1 or ±2 imbalance can be all it takes to make you a winner! Remember: traditional Basic Strategy just gives you about a 50/50 chance, with a random deck. If you learn to recognize Core imbalances and combine the correct strategy moves with them, you will become successful.

Personally, I prefer single- and double-deck games, with just two to four players in them. I don't even do much math—I just keep an informal count, watching closely for clumps and imbalances. The game moves quickly and always has a chance of being manipulated by a well-placed cut.

Bad decks are over in a couple of hands. The other side of this, that good decks end quickly also, is the reason why some people prefer shoes. A streak might last longer with a shoe. And, with shoes, usually all the cards are dealt face-up on the table.

If you play in Atlantic City, you'll find it difficult, if not impossible, to find anything but four-, six- and eight-deck shoes. A four-deck shoe can actually be a fairly quick moving game. A full table of six to seven players will usually receive about six to eight hands before the next shuffle.

Tip #2: Anytime that your Core count (or Real ratio) returns to "0" you can start your count over, even if you're in the same shoe. Zero means that the remaining deck has the normal amount of Core cards in it. Therefore, you can start tracking as if you're at the top of a (temporarily) smaller shoe.

STEPS TO THE CORE RATIO

1) Learn to count from 0 to 128 by fours. (See Table #7)

2) Learn to think of decks by quarters.

3) Learn to eyeball the sizes of remaining shoes or decks.

4) Know how many decks and Core cards are in your game before starting play.

5) Learn to calculate the Real Ratio. Formula:

(a) Multiply the surplus (+) or deficit (−) number of Core cards by four.

b) Divide that number by the (numerator of) the amount of quarter decks that remain.

6) Whenever the Core count reaches "0," simply start over, for increased accuracy.

7) Remember, if you lose count, that informal counts can often be virtually as effective. Sloppiness, of course, can cause disaster. Spot the trends. Relaxed Vigilance.

8) Always be aware of clumping, if it's present.

Chapter 6.

Cashing In On A Core Meltdown

Imagine a deck that is all and nothing but the Core. It would provide a nightmare of a game. Think of it. A deck composed entirely of fives, sixes, sevens and eights.

All your two-card hands would total between ten and sixteen. Your best hope for a double down would be hitting hard eleven with an eight, for nineteen, and that would be rare. You'd probably hit like crazy, because the dealer would show a five or six half of the time. Overall, the game would be a laborious battle of inferior hands, with very little busting, and the side that happened to get up to any standing hand would usually be the winner. If you knew that the Core was solid, you'd be wise to keep your bets down, while playing in a mush of a game worse than a mudhole. Why bother? It's better just to leave.

What's the other side of this? When the Core becomes so light that it disappears? What I call a Core Meltdown. That's when the deck gets hot!

Now you're in a game that consists of only the cards two, three and four combined with nine, ten and ace.

Your two-card hands would show some fours through eights, more twelves, thirteens and fourteens, and many nineteens, twenties and blackjacks. Your only fifteens would be soft. Busting would abound—dealer busting

69

TABLE #10

A CORE Meltdown

Second card

First Card	2	3	4	5	6	7	8	9	T	T	T	T	A
2	4	5	6					11	12	12	12	12	3/13
3	5	6	7					12	13	13	13	13	4/14
4	6	7	8					13	14	14	14	14	5/15
5													
6													
7													
8													
9	11	12	13					18	19	19	19	19	10/20
T	12	13	14					19	20	20	20	20	BJ
T	12	13	14					19	20	20	20	20	BJ
T	12	13	14					19	20	20	20	20	BJ
T	12	13	14					19	20	20	20	20	BJ
A	3/13	4/14	5/15					20	BJ	BJ	BJ	BJ	2/12

Only four cards (less than a third) are missing from the deck, but over half the possible hands are gone (88/169) are missing.

BET UP!

38/81 hands (46.9%) will be Blackjack, twenty, nineteen or hard eleven, with a two out of three chance for a good hit, or (9,9) or (A,A) with almost a two out of three chance for a good hit.

34/81 will be nineteen and up (42%-more than double a normal deck)

8/81 will be Blackjack (9.9%-more than double the normal deck)

28/81 will be hard stiffs 12–14 (34.6%-slightly down from a normal deck)

would rise past 40%. The unfortunate player that wasn't aware that the Core had completely disappeared would probably end up taking a lot of bad hits, since the dealer would show nine or more two-thirds of the time, or they'd see themselves receive many good hands (nineteen and up), possibly without having any sizable bet out.

You, the Core player, however, when finding yourself in the presence of a Core Meltdown, should employ extreme methods of strategy.

Your bets should be high, because your chances for blackjack would be more than double, as would your chances for a nineteen or twenty.

Chances of two-card stiffs are slightly lower, and they would total only twelve through fourteen, but, if the dealer showed a two, three or four, you should always stand and let the glut of high cards work their probability of busting the dealer.

Your stiffs vs. dealer nine and ten would be more wisely surrendered*, because of that same high probability of a bust. Table #11 shows that it's not worth risking a hit when you have the advantage of taking half

TABLE #11

Third Card in A CORE Meltdown

Third Card

Two Card Total	2	3	4	5	6	7	8	9	T	T	T	T	A
4	6	7	8					13	14	14	14	14	5/15
5	7	8	9					14	15	15	15	15	6/16
6	8	9	10					15	16	16	16	16	7/17
7	9	10	11					16	17	17	17	17	8/18
8	10	11	12					17	18	18	18	18	9/19
9													
10													
11	13	14	15					20	21	21	21	21	2/12
12	14	15	16					21	B	B	B	B	13
13	15	16	17					B	B	B	B	B	14
14	16	17	18					B	B	B	B	B	15

$$14/81 = \text{Bust}$$
$$30/81 = \text{Hard Stiffs } 12–16$$
$$12/81 = \text{Hard 17 \& 18}$$
$$\text{Only } 7/81 = \text{19 or above}$$

*Surrender and insurance are discussed in Appendix B.

of your bet back. If you can't employ the surrender option, there is still no use risking a hit on your stiffs. Your only hope is that the dealer has one also, because the chance of bust is very high.

With dealer showing ace, it's usually not worth taking insurance*, since insurance pays only 2–1, and the odds are slightly higher: 9–4. If they fall to 8–4 or less, then do take it. And, if you believe that you're in a ten clump, then you should insure any hand, during the Core Meltdown, for there will be so many tens that you could cash in on that 2–1 payoff, instead of losing your bet to dealer blackjack.

Double down on your hard eights and elevens (there won't be any hard nines or tens) vs. Dealer two, three or four. Don't double down on anything else, no matter how good it looks.

The only pairs available will be 2,2; 3,3; 4,4; 9,9 and A,A. Split 9,9 and A,A vs. Dealer 2,3 and 4. Split 2,2 and 3,3 vs. Dealer 2 and 3. Continue to hit 4,4.

Cashing in on this rare phenomenon of the Meltdown is a possibility open only to the Core player. The Basic Strategist and the Ten Counter will raise their bets, but they'll double down too much and bust out on many of their stiffs. The regular player probably won't be aware that anything very exceptional is even taking place, until it's already over.

Sound crazy? Well, it's a Core Meltdown!

Chapter 7.

Core Training

Now you've seen *why* the CORE System works and *how* it works. And, if you're anything like me, you're probably impatient to try it out in a real game. Let me steer you in the right direction and make your job a little easier.

Remember a couple of things. The first is: Don't Get Greedy.

Most games swing back to the house after two to five wins. Be willing to settle for three to four wins at a sitting, especially when you're just starting to use this system. If you've won your three to four hands and haven't lost one yet, go ahead and play until the dealer wins. You might win nine or ten hands in a row, but these games are fairly rare.

When the day comes to a close you'll feel far better having won a few hands in a few games than *almost* having won a lot, but ending up having lost instead. Blackjack is, in a way, the experience of being surrounded by losing players. The pleasure of being ahead at the end of play, even if it's only by a few hands, instead of counting yourself in that great group of losers, is a tremendous source of strength and confidence.

The other side of Don't Get Greedy is: Learn To Limit Your Losses.

Don't make losing at a particular game a personal beef between you and the casino or dealer. Set a loss limit and, if your reach it, simply walk away. There are dozens, if not hundreds of other games to pick from. And usually, upon walking away and reflecting on what went wrong, you will notice something in the previous situation that you didn't recognize when you were actually at the table. Perhaps there was a Core imbalance, but the Core cards sat right in a clump of tens. Or, even though the Core cards were clumped together, somehow the shuffle always left them *in* the deck, instead of letting them get dealt out to create the Light Core that makes for good play. Or maybe you made some wrong strategy moves, etc.

My personal loss limit is five betting units. If I double down on my first bet and lose, I've already lost two betting units. If I do reach my loss limit I don't hesitate to walk away. At the time of this writing, I haven't lost more than four units at any sitting in the last two years. During that time I've improved my winning rate from about two of every three sittings (60–67%) up to four of every five sittings (80%).

The fact that my one losing game in five has been limited to no more than four units lost has, obviously, contributed greatly to my profits. I simply *don't stick around to lose.* If I lose, it's not a personal thing between the dealer or casino and me. Because I know that I'm good enough to get it back sooner or later. Maybe not in the same place, but sometime soon, somewhere.

And because I remember another thing: No matter how good you are, or how much you know, You Can't Win With A Losing Deck.

So, how do you spot a winning deck? I'll teach you what to look for, and I'll do this in two parts. Part I is some simple card reading exercises to teach you to rapidly read a deck. Part II will describe the ways that casinos set up decks, and how you can recognize them and use them to help you win.

I can't provide you with a list of good or bad casinos; conditions can change overnight, so anything I say could become quickly dated. There are publications that can keep you well-abreast of current casino conditions. Stanford Wong's *Current Blackjack News* (est. 1979) and Eddie Olsen's *Blackjack Confidential Magazine* (est. 1986) will both fill the bill nicely.* Both keep up with current dealing and shuffling techniques, as well as rule changes and profitable gimmicks that casinos sometimes offer. *Blackjack Confidential* also provides the monthly win percentages filed by the casinos with the New Jersey and Nevada State authorities. I've found, from reading these, that Downtown Las Vegas is usually the "easiest" place to win—that is, they usually have the lowest casino blackjack win percentages. I attribute this to the extremely competitive downtown situation. If you don't like one place, you can move to another right next door.

But, if you know what to look for, you can win anywhere that you recognize the right conditions. Spotting the right conditions isn't something that you do with a pen and paper, or by counting on your fingers while hiding them in your pockets. It's a technique, solid in basis, that takes the well-trained person seconds. It's done in a manner that doesn't appear to an on-looker, like any evaluation is taking place.

The ideal player, from the casino's viewpoint, is

Current Blackjack News, Pi Yee Press, 7910 Ivanhoe #34, La Jolla, CA, 92037-4511.

Blackjack Confidential Magazine, 513 Salsbury Rd., Cherry Hill, NJ, 08034.

someone that sits down at the first available seat and just takes their chances. Don't get off on the wrong foot by gawking at everyone's cards for hand after hand while not playing. One expensive system that I bought had players evaluating a minimum of ten hands before sitting down. If the dealer shuffled up, you stood around and waited through that, also. Why not just wear a sign announcing that you have a tracking system, and that you're not just an average player? Don't invite extra casino defenses before you even sit down.

The Core player keeps a low profile.

There *are* scouting techniques, such as the Hit-and-Run, which utilize a lot of helpful tips. In fact, the first real improvement in my game came when I started to spot signs, not in the cards, but around and at the tables, signs that indicated a probable winning situation. I'll outline some of these tips later and you may find them quite helpful.

It wasn't until I developed and started using the CORE System that I became a strong, top-notch player. Limiting my losses and playing only at tables that show certain deck structures, the kind that can produce a Light Core, I found that, in the long run, I'll come out ahead.

There are basically two types of decks you'll encounter. The first is the Balanced or Random Deck, a relative rarity. In its presence, use the traditional Basic Strategy moves. (Basic Strategy is the center portion of each of the Core Strategy Charts, in the Appendices.) Learn traditional Basic Strategy, for you'll use it whenever the Core count, or the Real Ratio, is at "0." Basic Strategy is mathematically sound *when applied at the proper time.* The big fallacy of Basic Strategy, and its accompanying

Ten Tracking principle, is that the casinos have defeated it by creating the Defensive Deck.

The Defensive Deck is the second type of deck. It has two sub-types: the Simple, and the Complex. The Simple type has clumps of large-valued cards alternating with clumps of medium- and/or small-valued cards. The second, more Complex type, is merely the mixing of those two clumps together, creating a high/low /high/low order. In a shoe game this high/low order might be mixed together with the other styles, that is, simple clumps and balanced decks. One type follows the other, maybe goes back to the first, then maybe there's a fairly well-balanced section. An eight-deck shoe can provide a real roller coaster of variation. But in the hand-held games you will generally see only one type of set-up. There simply aren't enough cards for more than that.

Once you learn to recognize the type of Defensive Deck that you're facing, you may, as I have been, be astonished that you've never noticed it before, or that the other people at the table still don't see what's going on. Here are some exercises, the first ones to help you learn to read decks more quickly, and the following ones to help you learn to recognize the two types of Defensive Decks.

Exercise #1: Obtain two brand new decks, each with a different backing, say, red and blue, or with different designs. Open the first one, remove the jokers and advertisements, and lay it out face-up, in a manner similar to that seen in a casino, i.e., a half-circle. (See Table #12).

Notice the ready-made clumps? These are present in every brand new deck. There are eight tens sitting right in the middle, with two groups of four tens each to the sides. Notice the clumps of low range (two through six) cards, four of four cards each. And the middle range cards, again four clumps of them. Of course, there are also four clumps of the five through eight Core cards.

Exercise #2: Take half of the newly opened deck that you've spread in front of you, separating it right at the two kings in the middle, so that you have twenty-six cards. Shuffle it thoroughly. Place that shuffled half deck in a pile, *face up,* in front of you. Open the other deck of cards, which has a different backing, remove the jokers and advertisements, and shuffle it thoroughly. Place it *face up* in front of you, also.

Without looking (close your eyes, if you have to), remove two cards from the full deck and place them at random into the shuffled half deck. Now, give the half deck another shuffle, *keeping it face up,* so you don't see the backs of the cards.

Next, simply take the face up half deck with the two new cards hidden in it and quickly scan through it, card by card, putting the discards into another face up pile. (Keep everything face up, get it?) Name the two additional values that have been added to the deck. There should be three of two denominations, or four of one denomination. Which is it? What are the new card values? You can find out if you've picked the right values by turning the deck over and finding the two cards that have the different backings.

Take out those two cards and repeat the exercise, adding two more cards, everything face up again. Find the two new cards again. Repeat the exercise two dozen more times, until the new deck with the different backing is used up. This exercise will teach you to quickly recognize simple card surpluses.

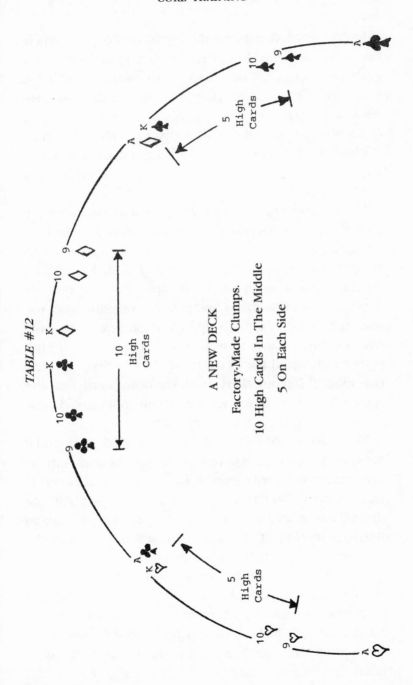

TABLE #12

A NEW DECK
Factory-Made Clumps.
10 High Cards In The Middle
5 On Each Side

10 High Cards

5 High Cards

5 High Cards

Exercise #3: Rearrange the cards to make two whole but separate decks. Remove eight ten-valued cards and two aces from each deck (a total of twenty cards) and place them in a separate pile. Shuffle the remaining two decks together. Give your pile of twenty aces and tens a quick shuffle, so that the backings get mixed together. Without looking, place the pile of twenty cards somewhere into your double deck, keeping the pile of twenty cards together.

Now, set up a game for four players and a dealer. Sit in one of the player's positions, so the exercise will look more like what you as a player will be seeing in a casino. If you wish, you can obtain chips and make bets for yourself and/or each player before you deal out the hands. Deal to first base (first player's) position first. You may keep all of the cards up, if you like, except for the dealer's down card. Now play out a few hands, until you've exhausted the deck. If the dealer shows an Ace, play everything out, then check the down card. If dealer turns out to have blackjack, cancel all splits and double downs, taking only the original bets.

The purpose of this exercise is two-fold. First, you'll see how a solid clump of tens performs. It's quite simple: everyone gets twenty except for possibly a lucky blackjack or two. Hopefully, one of those wasn't for the dealer, but it easily could be. Second, you'll begin to notice a section of the deck that just doesn't seem to have the high cards that you need for double downs, or for dealer busts. One part of the deck will provide a lot of pushes with the dealer at twenty (or a dealer blackjack, to wipe everyone out), the other will provide a hand for the dealer that hits once, twice, even three times without busting, until the dealer has a standing hand.

A clump doesn't have to be very large to affect a particular hand. Say that there are four players at the table. Five cards dealt give all players and the dealer their first card. Another five cards give everyone their second. If just eight of the ten cards are tens, either three or four of the participants *must* receive twenty. Keep in mind that it's not unusual for eight of ten cards to be tens in some part of a deck or shoe. Card clumps of twenty or more consecutive tens can and do happen.

This is how Simple Clumping functions in the Defensive Deck. If you don't know that it's coming, or you don't know the size of the clump, it can be quite devastating. To experience Complex Clumping, or the high/low/high/low order, and how that can throw off your game, try this next exercise.

Exercise #4: Pull out from your double deck the pile of twenty tens and aces. Pull out another twenty cards, all with a value of two through six. Put one pile of twenty cards on top of the other.

Now perform a "Strip Shuffle." To do this, make a second pile while holding your deck of forty in one hand and simultaneously taking one card from both the bottom and the top of the deck, placing those in a separate pile. You will see this "Strip Shuffle" quite often in casinos. Some use it as part of the House Shuffle. Others will pull it out when the table starts to win. And some places just instruct their dealers to "strip the deck" every three or four rounds, regardless. (More on shuffles in chapter ten.) Be aware that the Strip Shuffle encourages the high/low order.

Next, lightly shuffle your forty-card deck into a section of the rest of your double deck and start to play as before. When you get to the high/low section, you will notice a swing in favor of the house. If you stand, you'll probably be standing on a stiff; if you hit, you'll often bust. The dealer will usually show a Ten, encouraging players to hit and bust, or she'll show a low card, encouraging players to stand on their stiffs. Even though you know that you've created a forty-card section of high/low order, that one additional shuffle you gave it when you added it to the rest of the deck will make things so unsure that you'll probably notice the house starting to win most of the hands, *even when the dealer ends up busting.*

Why Clumping Occurs.

Remember how we created that forty-card high/low clump? We just combined a clump of tens with a clump of low cards. The two kinds of clumping, the Simple and the Complex, are encouraged by the way the cards are packaged, by the way the casinos prepare them for play, by various shuffles and post-play card pick-up techniques the dealers use *and by the game itself!*

Yes, the very play of blackjack encourages high-card clumping. The object of the game (to get the highest hand), and the decisions of the players to try to bring cards together that add up to higher and higher hands, tend to encourage the higher cards to clump together. Two-card high totals are left alone. Small pairs (8,8 and below) are split apart. When nine, ten or eleven are held, often only one more card is taken if the player believes that it will be high. In short, the players themselves help the high cards to come together.

The dealers also have a tremendous influence on how the cards will clump. Blackjacks are picked up right away and put into the discard pile. The rest of the cards stay on the table. When the hand is over, the dealer turns over all the cards to add up and double check the totals before she hands out pay-offs. Sometimes you'll notice her putting cards into certain orders, ostensibly to make totalling them easier, but, with the casino's blessing, she often places them in a more favorable order, as far as the house is concerned. Anything that the house allows, it does so because it believes that it will not be unfavorable for itself. The house will not knowingly hurt itself!

And this is the irony of the Defensive Deck! It certainly helps the house by defeating the Basic Strategy Player, the ten tracker and the Plus/Minus Counter. But the Core Player, by observing Light and Heavy Cores, and keeping a close eye on the type of clumping in the deck, will *benefit* from the Defensive Deck. This is because the Core Player tracks only *four medium-range* cards, the five, six, seven and eight.

Not only do the 5–8 cards have the biggest mathematical influence on the most frequent decisions of the game (in terms of depletions and surpluses), but the house simply doesn't pay as much attention to them. They can't. They already watch the tens and aces (that's five cards) to create Simple Clumps. When they create Complex Clumps, of the high/low nature, that usually involves another three or four lower-card values (making eight or nine cards). That leaves only four of the thirteen values of the deck. If they start messing with them, they'll be stacking the entire deck, and anyone who knows about it (like the readers of the CORE System) will be able to win.

How To Spot A Favorable Deck.

First, look for a Core imbalance.

Sometimes you will find all or some of the Core cards in some kind of clump. This is why Heavy and Light Cores occur. Remember, when the deck has a Heavy

Core, it puts you at a strategic disadvantage. And a deck with a Light Core puts you at a strategic advantage. Keep in mind that a deck with a Heavy Core at one end can turn it over with the shuffle and deal out those same cards, creating a Light Core for the next hands.

When you walk up to a table, take a quick look at the cards. If you don't want to linger, try to walk up at the end of the hand, when all of the cards are being turned over. If anyone questions you, you can say that you're waiting for the shuffle. Now, ask yourself what you're seeing.

First, do you see a lot of tens? Did everyone just push twenty with the dealer? That's a big Ten Clump. You may hear comments like, "This is like pushing back and forth in a mudhole," or "Win one, lose one."

Or are the tens alternating with low cards? Did most of the players already lose their hand by busting a stiff? (Their bet will be gone.) Then, did the dealer also bust? If she made her hand, are the remaining players holding two-card stiffs? Does the dealer have a ten card with a lower card, that she just hit for a standing hand? You're seeing a Complex, or high/low clump. You may hear comments like, "I knew she didn't have it! (but she made it anyway!)" or, "Oh, no! She did it (made 20, 21) again!" or, simply, "She's too hot for me!"

Do you see *any* tens? If not, you may have very well just come during one of the lower clumps. The tens are probably packed together in some other part of the deck. You might hear comments like: silence, or groaning, as the dealer just took two, three or four hits to make a standing hand. Most of the players will have stiffs. There might be only one ten on the table, if that many.

All of (but not only) the above three situations could be favorable for the Core player. If you see any of the above, you should then ask yourself, Do I see either a lot of, or, almost no Core cards? Either case could mean the presence of a Core imbalance. And that is what we want to find. Because a Heavy Core on one shuffle can easily turn into a Light Core the next.

Even if you haven't had time to actually observe enough of the deck, learn to spot the trademarks of a Core imbalance. Ask yourself, "Am I seeing a lot of fifteens, sixteens, seventeens, and eighteens (signs of a Heavy Core)? Or am I seeing a lot of twelves, thirteens and fourteens (signs of a possible Light Core)? Am I seeing lots of double downs taking bad hits (possible Heavy Core)? Or, do I see only a few double downs, which are getting good hits (possible Light Core)?"

Memorize the traits listed in Table #2 and learn to spot them. Most players attribute those types of things to luck, but you, as a Core Player, can learn to see signposts in them.

Here, once again, is a more simple listing of the procedure for finding a favorable deck:

1) Determine if you're in the presence of a Balanced or a Defensive Deck.

2) If it's Defensive, what kind of clumping are they using, Simple or Complex?

3) If it's Complex, see if the lower part of the high/low scheme uses mostly Core cards or mostly lower valued cards (two, three and four). Avoid it if it uses too many 5–8 Core cards.

4) Determine if there is a Core imbalance. You don't have to see all four Core card values. A cluster of fives

and sevens, or sixes and eights will do. Or, as well, a marked absence of fives, sixes, sevens and/or eights.

5) Learn the traits, as outlined in Table #2, of the Heavy and Light Cores in play.

If the deck meets these criteria, then watch for just one more thing in the deck structure: Make sure that it doesn't have a Heavy Core mixed in with a strong clump of tens. A clump of tens combined with a clump of Core cards is a *player-killing* game!

And remember: It only takes a shuffle and/or a well-placed cut to make a Core flip over and become its opposite. Light to Heavy. Heavy to Light.

You respond to this by changing the size of your wager. That's why we next have a chapter on betting.

Chapter 8.

Betting and Bankroll

If the Core of the deck is like the steering wheel of a car, then betting can certainly be likened to the gas pedal.

As a player, you have a number of advantages. You can pick any table, at any time, in any casino. You can leave the game whenever you wish. And you can bet up when the game's good, down when it's bad.

This last advantage, bet variation, can offer you incredible control in your game. By changing the size of your bet, you can effectively respond to many of the curves and home runs that blackjack can throw at you. Bet variation is a very potent tool. When mishandled, it can destroy you. It can make you a loser, even though you've won most of your hands.

The other side of the coin: You can end up a winner, even though you've lost most of your hands.

There are two considerations when it comes to the topic of betting:

1) Size of the Basic Betting Unit.

2) Spread of the Betting Ratio.

The Betting Unit. Let's address #1, the size of your betting unit. It's easier to think and talk about blackjack bets in terms of "units." A "betting unit" is simply the amount, however much, that you wager if you feel that you're betting on a deck that is normal, or balanced, at the moment of the bet. The amount you'd bet when the

Real Ratio, or Core Count, is at "0," even if you know that there's an imbalance somewhere in the cards up ahead.

By basing your betting unit on a normal deck, it allows you to retreat, or reduce your bet size, in the presence of a Heavy Core, and to increase it, or raise, when there's a Light Core. Changing your bet size in response to strategic advantage or disadvantage (betting up when the game's good, down when it's bad) is the basis of the most successful gambling systems, no matter what the game.

The secret of successful betting is to bet in relation to your bankroll. Put another way: Don't gamble with money that you can't afford to lose.

I used to scoff at that idea, telling myself that I really didn't care whether or not I lost some of the rent money, because some more would come along sometime, somehow. But, as I got better at my game, and therefore, more sensitive to what was making it tick, I began to notice that the pressure of possibly losing money that I couldn't really afford to lose was actually *influencing my decisions.* I did not play as well with the extra pressure that I was putting on myself. So, I stopped playing with money that I couldn't afford to lose.

To my great surprise, I found that I actually gained strength from this policy. The new knowledge that, even if I lost every cent of my bankroll, nothing in my life would change, because I played only with money that I could afford to lose, turned me into a relaxed, unpressured player. There was no way that the casino could hurt me! They could take my money, but it was money that I was now mentally prepared to lose, if it came to that. Nothing in my life would change if I lost.

On the other hand, I knew that I now had an even

stronger possibility of winning, because I could think more clearly, and because I was enjoying myself more. This may seem elementary to most of you, but some of us just have to learn it the hard way. It's a lesson that you should never forget.

Okay, let's say that you're planning a trip to Nevada, and you know that after all the travel expenses, food, room, gas, etc., you'll have $1,000 left to devote to the games. Are you going to play only blackjack? Probably not. If you're like most players, you'll play at least one other game. Even professional gamblers usually have another game that they play for relaxation. The fact that you're probably going to play another game while you're there makes it wise to deduct that amount of monies from what you ultimately consider your blackjack bankroll. Likewise, don't put unnecessary pressure on yourself by using room, food or gas money.

If I have $1,000, I know that I'll want to visit the craps tables a couple times, with $200 in my pocket each time. That's $400. I know that I'll want to buy a few rolls of silver dollars for the slots and some quarter rolls for those silly video keno machines. That's another $100. So, I know that $500 of my $1,000 will go for other games. That still leaves me $500 to bet on my primary game, blackjack. What should the size of my betting unit be?

Speaking for myself, I would make my betting unit $15, with a $500 bankroll.

$500 ÷ $15 = 33 betting units (with $5 left over)

Since I make it a practice never to let myself lose more than five units at any one table, I know that I can lose five games in a row and still have enough units to play a sixth. And since I've honed my game to produce a win rate of four of every five games, I can play in a relaxed fashion, confident that they *probably* won't beat me six times before I can beat them once. This knowledge lets me relax, and, therefore, I play better.

With my $15 basic unit, I know that I'll be able to retreat to a $10 bet when the deck gets bad, and that I'll be able to raise up to $20 when it gets good. I am a good player and I still give myself the padding of a thirty-three-unit bankroll. Anything can happen in gambling! Even with a win rate of 80%, I accept the fact that it's still possible for me to lose all of my money.

But even if you don't win 80% of the time, or even half of the time (yet), you can improve your results by following this simple advice: Don't Stick Around To Lose! Decide on a stop/loss point before you sit down and don't go past it. This will improve your discipline, it will let you have time to figure out, in a leisurely fashion, just what went wrong, and it will leave you money to try again.

If you are just starting out, either learning the game of blackjack, or trying out the CORE System for the first time, I would strongly recommend that you divide your bankroll by at least fifty units ($500 ÷ 50 = $10 per unit) or even 100 units ($500 ÷ 100 = $5 per unit). And, whether or not you consider yourself a beginner, you must be mentally prepared to accept that you can lose every cent.

Don't make the mistake that bigger bets will somehow give you a better chance at winning. Any hand at which you lose $5 will still be a losing hand, even if you had bet $5,000. But, for some reason, there are still people that think that they'll do better if they bet bigger. Many claim that if they make bigger bets, then they'll have to win only two or three hands to make some real money. This is an illusion. You can't let the size of your bet make you sweat, or it will influence your decisions and your game. I'll illustrate this with a personal experience.

I walked up to a two-deck game, noticing that there was a nice clump of tens at one end of the deck and a Heavy Core at the other end. There were already four other players at the table, but the dealer was dealing low enough into the deck to insure that there were two hands per shuffle. It seemed like I could work the CORE System there, so I sat down. On my immediate right, at first base, stood a guy in a business suit with five piles of green chips ($25 each) in front of him. Each pile had $200 in it. The table limits were $10–$200. The guy held a drink, obviously not his first, while his wife stood silently behind, as if tolerating a familiar situation.

My basic betting unit was $15, but I knew we were into the Heavy Core, so I bet $10. The guy on my right put up $150. He won. I lost. The dealer shuffled. The next hand I bet $15. He bet $200.

"Maximum bet!" yelled the dealer over her shoulder. The guy swelled with pride as the pit boss glanced over, calling back "Okay!" The suit got dealt a fourteen, I a twelve. He stood, while I hit my twelve with a seven, recognizing that we were again into the Heavy Core of the deck (extra 5–8s), and ended up with nineteen. The dealer hit her stiff for a standing hand 18. I collected $15, first base lost $200. The deck was into the Ten Clump, with a now Light Core.

We each got twenties to the dealer's nineteen. He collected $100, I $20. When he put out a $200 bet, the dealer called out "Maximum bet!" as she shuffled up. He nodded knowingly, causing the sweat to glisten on his brow, then busted hitting a stiff. I pushed, keeping my $10. We were into the Heavy Core, and I'd kept my bet low. He pushed out another $200. This time he stood on his stiff. I hit mine successfully, collecting $10 when the dealer hit her stiff, but for a lower total. The guy looked unhappy pushing out another $200. The dealer shuffled and dealt stiffs. He busted his. I stood. Dealer busted. I collected $15.

The guy with the big bankroll had just lost three $200 bets.

He shrugged and put out a $10 bet, I a $20 bet. We were into a rich ten/ace clump with a Light Core. I wanted to tell him that now was a good time to bet maximum, but I know not to give advice at the tables. The guy got dealt a blackjack and was paid $15. He threw up his hands in disgust, then pushed out $200.

"Maximum bet!"

We're into the Heavy Core, I would have liked to warn him, but I kept my mouth shut. I bet $10. The guy stood on his stiff. I hit mine successfully. So did the dealer, taking the other fellow's $200.

Things continued in this fashion. The gutsy guy's piles of green chips were all gone. He pulled out two one-hundred-dollar bills and lost those. Then he left. We avoided each other's eyes. I quit the game a few minutes later. I was $45 ahead. Who do you think felt better—the big loser or me with my $45 win?

Moral: Don't let other players, or dealers, or yourself, goad you to bet beyond your means. Even if you can afford larger bets, if they make you uncomfortable, they will only make you play worse. *Bets that make you sweat will affect your ability to make good decisions.*

The size of the betting unit is only the first half of this explosive ingredient of the game. The second part, betting ratio, is more important.

Bet Ratio (Betting Spread).

Betting Ratio is just another term for the "range" of your bet sizes. It's also known as the "spread." Casinos won't be happy with a spread of more than about 5:1 or 6:1. The casinos know that bet size isn't nearly as important as the betting spread.

In my case, my betting unit is often $15. I can retreat to $10 with a Heavy Core, and raise to $20 with a Light Core. Therefore, my betting spread is $10–$20, a 2:1 ratio. This is small, but very effective. It means that for every two bets that I lose when betting $10 during a Heavy Core, I only have to win one when betting $20 during a Light Core. Theoretically, I could lose two of three bets and still end up even. But, since I win about half of my lower Heavy Core bets, and more than half of my larger Light Core bets, I usually do quite nicely.

This gives me a very unthreatening betting profile. Furthermore, since I lose about half of the smaller bets (made during strategic disadvantage) and I often have occasion, if the Core lightens up, to raise my bet for the next hand, I take on the profile of a "bet chaser," which the casinos usually love. Another advantage of my betting style is, in winning most of my larger bets, I can lose 60% of my hands and still walk away a winner.

Gambling is a two-edged sword—anything can happen. Just because you've learned the CORE System well, and make it a point to raise only in the presence of a Light Core, doesn't guarantee you the win. And if you make your Light Core bets too high, trying to extend your spread, and you end up losing, you can wipe out a half a dozen hard won smaller bets. Remember: It takes more than guts to be a steady winner at the tables.

Here is the basic Core betting plan:

Ratio (Spread)—2:1 or 3:1

Basic betting unit: Your average bet. The bet that you make when the Core count is "0," or when the deck is balanced. The smallest bet is 50% smaller than your average bet. Your biggest bet is 50% larger than your average bet.

Heavy Core: $1/2$ betting unit

Normal deck: 1 betting unit

Light Core: $1\frac{1}{2}$ betting units

With this plan you never do more than triple your bet.

If you run into a game where the dealer just can't seem to stop busting, or where you just can't seem to stop winning, wait until you've gotten ahead four or five hands before you raise the size of your basic betting unit. Then raise it just 30–40–50%, to some round number that is easy to make with your chips. If you're betting $5 and you've won five hands in a row and are well ahead, obviously you can't move up to $7.50. They won't let you bet the 50¢. Don't go right up to $10. Just go up to $7 or $8. If you continue to win, say, another three hands, then raise your basic unit up to $10. Keep it simple and conservative.

Sometimes, in the heat of play, you may find that you have trouble figuring out just how many hands you've actually won or lost. There is an easy, traditional method for keeping track of this. Simply use some extra chips and every time that you win a hand, put a chip in one pile. Every time that you lose a hand, put a chip in another pile. When the piles become too big, figure the

difference in chips between the two piles, leave those
extra chips on the table and remove the rest. Then start
your win/lose piles from there. The remaining chips will
already mark your net win or loss up to that point. That
will be one of your new win/loss piles. This is a good
idea, because it leaves your mind free for other matters
in the game.

Warning: Never throw the end of your bankroll into
one last big bet. You must always be prepared to handle a
split or double down opportunity. Who wants to be
caught with an (8,8) or an (A,A), and have no more
money with which to split it?

Chapter 9.

Core Discipline

(MANNERS AT THE TABLE)

As a Core player, you will have the advantage of stepping out of the established profiles. You won't always bet or take hits like the normal player or the average Ten Counter. This will work to your favor. But counters and card trackers can give themselves away a number of other ways.

How Counters Give Themselves Away:

—By being overly chatty; displaying false familiarity. One should not advertise how much time one has spent at the tables, by trying to be suave and experienced, or by showing how clever and witty one can be.

—By somber appearance, as if thinking deeply about something—usually counting.

—By hesitating, then acting like they're trying to remember what to do with an uncommon hand or difficult situation, sometimes coupled with muttering, "Now what do I do here?"

—By paying overt attention to the cards at the end of a hand, as the dealer turns them up.

—By pulling back large bets when the dealer shuffles up.

The best profile is a low profile. Second best is when some noisy person or know-it-all actually draws attention away from you. Unfortunately, they sometimes draw unwanted attention to the table.

Don't instruct others.

Don't annoy the dealer. Of course, some dealers are just crabby. You shouldn't take it personally. After all, you can leave anytime. Sometimes it may seem that a dealer is unfriendly. If that bothers you, then just walk away. The same goes if other players annoy you. A cigarette in your face. An obnoxious drunk. Body odor. If it's really such a bother that it's affecting your game, simply depart. Stay loose; don't let minor irritations make you a bad player.

Don't let another player's wrong moves bother you. My philosophy is that an unpredictable player is usually no different than an extra shuffle to the deck. However, if I run into a player who seems to always be taking the dealer's bust card, or somehow is losing hand after hand for the table, I walk away.

A good mental exercise is to remember good plays that you've made. It will help turn you into a positive, success-oriented player.

The Pit Boss.

Players who are intimidated by the pit boss are overreacting. They don't understand the pit boss's role. He or she (they come in all sizes, shapes and tempers) is there to keep the dealers and players honest, to make sure that the playing atmosphere is pleasant and to settle disagreements. In Nevada, they are also on the lookout for card counters.

Avoid too much eye contact with the pit bosses, but don't skulk in reaction to them. Furtive behavior will attract attention. Relax, but don't get sloppy.

A pit boss's presence isn't necessarily directed towards you. If the table starts paying out, they will gravitate there to make sure that all exchanges are correct. Less experienced dealers may need more attention from the pit, as well.

The pit boss has to stand somewhere. If they choose to stand next to you, it may not mean anything. I've had very pleasant conversations with some pit bosses. They are the best people in the casino to answer questions that you might have. Occasionally, to lower my profile, I might even ask the pit boss, if he's right there, next to me, whether he thinks I should stand or draw on my hand.

But even the friendliest pit boss will act decisively if they think that they are in the presence of a cheater. And, in Nevada, card trackers are considered cheaters. How can you tell if the pit boss is developing suspicions towards you and your card tracking system?

Most commonly, they will watch your eyes.

They, or the dealer, may also check your betting style, your strategy moves, watch to see if you pull back a big bet when the dealer shuffles up, or just your general demeanor at the table (thus, we have this chapter on manners at the table). But the most common thing that they will do, if they're really interested in you, is watch your eyes.

They want to see how much attention that you pay to other players' cards especially at the end of the hands, when all of the cards get turned over. Sometimes, if you're playing first or third base (the end positions), they may stand right at the edge of your visual periphery, either just in or out of your sight. Perhaps they'll let you see their hands, placing them right next to you. And they watch your eyes.

Are you making quick, nervous glances in their direction? Do you, however quickly, make sure to catch sight of the cards at the end of the hand?

If I sense this scrutiny directed towards me, I may, between hands, simply gaze in a disinterested fashion out towards the rest of the casino. Anywhere but at the cards. I will ignore other people's cards during play. I may make a strategy move that is completely out of step with traditional Basic Strategy. (Sometimes I can do this and still be following the Core Strategy, a most satisfying moment.) These things are usually adequate to dispel any interest in my direction. Some people pull the drunk act, but that's been overdone.

Be forewarned that bet size has little to do with whether or not you get scrutinized. If they believe you are tracking cards, they will not take well to it.

I know one person, an expert Ten Counter, who regaled me with a tale of the first time that he got kicked out of a casino. "I felt like I had finally graduated!" he chortled. This is an improper attitude. You do not want to get on the lists of known counters. It would certainly be a Pyrrhic victory at best, for you'd find yourself being asked to leave many casinos.

Resorting to disguises is not a practical alternative. It is said that expert counter Ken Uston's early death was caused by complications following a parking lot beating he received after trying one too many times to sneak into casinos "undercover."

Some casinos can't seem to tolerate winners. They would remove the Invisible Man if too many chips started to accumulate in front of his empty suit.

Get confidence in your game and proper behavior

will naturally follow. The need to impress those around you is a symptom of a lack of confidence.

Drinking.

Don't depend on alcohol to provide you with confidence. Anyone who has had some drinks while gambling is familiar with the unpredictable impulses that come over a player that is intoxicated. You cannot both win and drink consistently.

If you must have alcohol sometime during the day, then do your serious blackjack playing early, before you drink. I find many uncrowded, choice tables during the early part of the day.

I am not going to lay a guilt trip on you. If you must have a drink as soon as you wake up, then I say this: The hour will come when you want to win more than you want that drink.

If you order a drink at the tables and you decide to leave, there is no rule that says that you have to stay until that drink comes. If you feel bad about it, you can still leave the game, stand near the tables and keep an eye out for your order.

When I'm in a casino for an extended length of time, the cocktail waitresses usually stop filling my orders (for sodas, juices, coffees), partially because I move around so much and I'm not there when they arrive. And it's partially because they take so long to bring them, in a transparent ploy to try to keep me at the table. Even if I stay in one spot, rarely have I had a drink delivered within a reasonable period of time. The drinks are just part of a plan to keep you at the tables longer and to cloud your judgment when you consume them.

Most casino bars will give you drinks for free if you

buy a roll of quarters or dollars. Some insist that you sit at the bar and play the video games, others make you pay for all drinks. Even if this last is the case, you'll probably find it cheaper in the long run. An even easier policy is to play, then drink.

Breathing.

It may seem ironic, but, as I look back over my extensive blackjack studies, I believe that some of the most valuable advice I ever received was to remember to BREATHE AT THE TABLES.

Some casinos are very crowded and smokey. Even if they're not, the position that one must assume, sitting, hunched up in a high chair, leaning on the tables, causes a person to breathe more and more shallowly. This cuts the flow of oxygen to your brain and also increases tension, both of which detract from your game.

I find it indispensable to periodically take deep breaths (silently), the kind where I move my stomach muscles. This works wonders. To get rid of additional stress, I find it helpful to squeeze my hand into a hard fist for a few seconds, then let go.

Along with these concepts, I advise you not to play when you're feeling badly, i.e., headache, upset stomach, depression, extreme fatigue, etc. These extra burdens will detract from your game.

The Double Down Card.

I have a personal test that keeps me aware of my stress and discipline levels.

When I double down on a hand and receive the double down card, I make myself refrain from turning it over until I see what the dealer's outcome is. No matter how anxious I am to see it, I keep myself from looking at it until I have to. (Many times it turns out that I didn't even have to see it, because the dealer ends up busting.

Dealer busting is a great stress reliever.) If I find that I simply cannot keep myself under control and must look at the card too soon, I know that it's a sign that my discipline and control is eroding.

Tipping The Dealer.

Everything in the casino is structured in a severe, robotic pyramid scheme. At the top is an almost mythical, never seen, ever receiving, ever watching, never feeling, fabulously fortunate, unmagnanimous and closely guarded entity, who is protected by a legal paper wall, an armed force, one-way mirrors and electronic security systems which equate pit bosses, dealers, and cocktail waitresses, janitors, winners, losers, high rollers, low renters, locals and you as potential but necessary threats.

You, the player, are at the bottom of a very tall pyramid into the clouds. As a dangling expendable appendage, you're as desirable as a dancer's boyfriend at a strip bar, as necessary, yet replaceable, to the casino's economics as a fly is to the food chain.

Taken in this light, questions such as "Should I tip the dealer?" become totally, thoroughly and utterly meaningless. Tip if you want to; don't if you don't.

To become a winning player, you must have the patience to find the right tables. You must learn to recognize the trends in the deck and remember the right moves for the situations that confront you. You must have the patience to observe your stop/loss limit, and to take losses in stride so that you can learn from them. You must refrain from making large bets until you find yourself winning more times than you're losing.

Patience and observation are the keys to sharpening your game.

Chapter 10.

Casino Defenses or Casino Cheating?

People sometimes cheat. Casinos are run by people. Therefore, casinos sometimes cheat.

A casino that takes some defensive counter-measures against winning players isn't cheating. A prevalent complaint I hear is that the shuffles and structures of today's Defensive Deck is no different than just stacking the deck (in other words, cheating). I don't agree. The people who run casinos are no different than you. They want to utilize defenses against their opponent, defenses that will help them win. If that means shuffling differently or changing the decks, then so be it! All of the Ten Counters, crying because somebody took away their lollipop, should wake up to the real world. Nobody owes you a living at cards!

This brings us to our next question: Is counting cards cheating?

According to the New Jersey Supreme Court, judging a case filed by Ken Uston, casinos there have no right to discriminate against card counters by preventing them from playing. To defend themselves, the casinos there now hardly ever offer a game with less than four decks.

On the other hand, the Nevada State Supreme Court responded to Uston by saying that their resort and hotel industry has a right to protect itself when its livelihood

105

is being threatened. As with many issues in the law, things then begin to get obscure. The court didn't specify counters, but the issue was brought up in superstar counter Ken Uston's Nevada discrimination lawsuit, so an argument could be made that the courts believed that card counters could be a threat. Certainly, by leaving it up to the Nevada casinos, they must have realized that would be the practical outcome of their decision.

The absurd obscurity of the issue arises when you ask: How does someone not count cards and still play a game where they have to add up values of cards to get as close to twenty-one as possible, basing actions partially on what they believe the value of the dealer's down card might be, and then, after the hand's over, estimate the size of their next bet on what they think their chances are of getting close to twenty-one, with the cards remaining in the deck? If it sounds confusing, it's no wonder! At what point does thinking about cards become systemizing them?

The casinos might reply: We know what a system is, and so do you, and if you're using a card tracking system in Nevada, you'll have to leave. But, we love systems players, and we'll send out a cab to the airport to pick them up!

The fact of the matter is, if they allowed counters and trackers to openly ply their trade in Nevada, then we probably wouldn't see many one- and two-deck games. So, I guess you can't have your cake and eat it, too. My advice is, if you want to use a tracking system in Nevada, then keep it low profile and, when it's working for you, don't get greedy with it. The casino's say it's cheating, but the courts didn't.

I've never been asked to leave a Nevada blackjack table, but I know others who have been. Some of them weren't even counting, were even behind over $100 and had never changed the size of their bet! That's the way the situation stands now—take it or leave it.

This isn't the only shadow region we find in the casino. There are other defenses where we begin to see an obscurity between the ethical and the unethical.

Deck Stacking.

For instance, we've spoken of how the casinos have decided to combat Ten Trackers by encouraging and enlarging the card clumps that come prepackaged in new decks. Even when they wash the cards (putting new decks face-down in a big pile on the table and mixing them loosely around), they don't do it very thoroughly, so as not to destroy those clumps. Is this cheating? I don't think so. Any new deck has clumps, and you should bear it in mind whenever the pit boss sticks new decks in the game. Player and dealer breaking usually tends to pick up with a new deck, and more split opportunities will appear, because of like-card clumping.

How about if they go through the decks and separate them into three piles, for instance, the 2–5s, the 6–tens and the jacks, queens, kings and aces, before they begin to shuffle them? Is this cheating? Yes, I believe it is. I believe that the state gambling commissions would frown on this. With this, they are beginning to stack the deck.

What about leaving all the cards on the table until the end of the hand, to preserve the structure of the deck? Is that cheating? No, of course not. How about when the dealer changes the order of the cards in each hand before she puts them back into the deck? Is that cheating? I believe it is. She's looking at the cards, face-up, and rearranging them, often to encourage a high/low/high/low order.

Shills.

How about a place that uses shills? Is that cheating? This is where things get really obscure.

A shill is an employee of the house who takes the position of a player in the game. Sometimes a shill is no more than a starter for the house, someone to draw some interest into the game when it just opens.

Shills can be fun to watch, for their play helps the house to lose as often as it helps it to win. Shills are quite legal and, if you keep your eyes open, you will see the number and letter of the law posted around various casinos, including the information that a shill must identify him or her self when asked.

How about if a shill starts to track cards for the house. How about if the dealer does? Is that cheating? Well, if you don't think it's cheating for *you* to track cards, how can it be for someone else to do the same? On the other hand, if the casinos have card-counting dealers, how can they expect us to sit still for it, if they won't let us do it?

Pressure On Dealers To Win.

Some places, more than others, tend to put more pressure on their dealers to perform well for the house. They do this because they know that there are things dealers can do to make it harder for you to win. The places where you encounter the feeling that the dealer is under pressure to win are often the same places that tend to come up with more defensive measures against players. Remember, a defensive measure isn't necessarily cheating.

The two most common measures, dealing the cards faster, and not dealing as deeply into the deck, can hardly be called unethical. Almost as common: different, more complex shuffles; new decks; new dealers. If these things start happening to you, you should be ready to leave in the case that they happen to be effective. You may wish to lower your bet while you determine if they are. These casino defenses are simple, but, often useful steps that, if it was *your* money being paid out, you would probably take also.

Of course, if the dealer is shuffling up after dealing out just one hand each time, and you still keep winning, you'll hardly have to worry about being accused of card counting. Replacing the decks usually tends to follow this last defense.

You should, however, keep an eye on the types of shuffles that the dealer uses. If you've been winning and the dealer suddenly changes her style of shuffling, you should proceed with caution, and be ready to leave if the winning stops. Keep in mind that some houses tell the dealer to use a different shuffle every three times or so, and it may have nothing to do with who's winning.

Probably the two most dangerous shuffles, in terms of disturbing the structure of a favorable deck, are "picking the deck" and the "strip shuffle."

Picking the deck is simply a procedure where the dealer gives special attention to sections of the shoe or deck that she believes show too much favor to the player. She may mix in other parts of the deck with it, or she may try to disperse it into the remaining cards. It can be effective. Some houses actually have the dealer track sections of the shoe by using chips, one color meaning "good" for the house, another color "bad." Then she can single out sections of the shoe for special shuffling attention.

Stripping the deck is a procedure, common in casinos, by which the dealer simultaneously removes the top and bottom card from the deck, or portion of it, and puts them into another pile. It's usually done very rapidly. Not only good for restructuring a winning deck, it is quite effective for creating the high/low order that destroys the logic behind Basic Strategy.

Many people have the misconception that stripping the deck merely reverses the order of the cards. This isn't true. To see what it really does, simply get ten cards, from ace (low) through ten, and put them in numerical order in a small pile. They will read A,2,3,4,5,6,7,8,9,10. Now, simultaneously remove the top and bottom cards and place them into a new pile. Do this for all ten cards. The order of the cards is now A,10,2,9,3,8,4,7,5,6. They are now in high/low/high/low order. If you see the "strip shuffle" suddenly appear where you haven't seen it before, and you've been winning, you should sit up and take notice.

There have been players that have made careers out of tracking shuffles. The basic principle is to remember the sections of a deck, or, more often, a shoe that has been particularly good or bad. Chips of different colors are piled up to indicate how well or poorly a section of the shoe behaved. Sometimes a third color will be used to track the neutral sections. Shuffle-tracking never got very popular because of all the variables that can get in the way.

The Mechanic.

"Mechanic" is a slang word for an expert card dealer or player. Even though not all casino mechanics are

cheaters, the word does have the connotation of someone who can take a game apart and put it back together
so it works better (for the house).

Almost all casinos have dealers that have a bit of
seniority, based on their winning power and their ability
to work with the management. You don't have to be
suspected of card-counting to warrant the services of
one of these "recovery experts." They are usually called
in simply to help the house recover some of its losses at a
dropping table. If you've been winning, and the dealer
suddenly changes, even though it doesn't seem to be
normal break time (dealers break every thirty to forty-
five minutes, usually), you should be alert for additional
casino defenses to appear.

The first of these defenses is usually dealing the cards
faster. Then they might change the decks on you,
opening up new ones. *Sometimes,* this increases breaking activity, which, if the rest of the table cooperates,
allows you to put the onus on the dealer to make her
hand.

New decks almost always increase clumping activity. I
once split four eights in a two-deck game that had just
introduced new decks. I hit them all, receiving sevens
on each one. On the third one I took an extra hit, getting
a queen and busting out. I was at third base and the
dealer showed a queen. She turned over a three, for
thirteen, hit it with a queen and busted. Any one of my
sevens or eights would have given her twenty or twenty-
one. The dealer was very unhappy, because that particular place put pressure on the dealers to win, and the pit
boss had already given her the new decks to stop the
table from dropping. There was a shill at the table,
wearing the casino's logo on his jacket, who showed

obvious disgust at my continuing success. A waitress whispered to him.

"Learning to count cards, eh, Frank?" he called to me.

I was staying at their motel and he'd just been told my name. I certainly wasn't going to call back that, No, I wasn't counting, but that new decks encourage like-card clumping. I played a few more hands, until the new decks started to take their toll, and I left.

I provide this illustration to show you that there are numerous defenses available to the casino before they even call in the Mechanic. Their purpose is to throw you off balance, to break your rhythm, to make you have to think and play faster, even to try to goad you into a personal war with the casino or the dealer. They realize that any of these things will usually make someone play worse. You may not realize everything that they did to you until you leave the game and think back on it. Then you may feel like you've been played for a sucker, but you should also realize that none of the above defenses were cheating.

Dealing Seconds.

There is something that some Mechanics do that definitely is cheating. It's called *dealing seconds.* Dealing seconds is a broad term that covers any movement that delivers an alternate card from another part of the deck than off the top, or bottom.

The term "dealing seconds" originally came from a trick movement that involved two steps. The first was when the dealer simply peeked at the top card before she took it. If it wasn't any good, she'd deal herself the one under it, figuring that the risk was less with an unknown card than a known bad one. One giveaway to "dealing seconds" was the "whishh" the cards made when the second card slipped out from between the others. To counter this, practices were developed which have lasted to this day, and which remain very good tip-offs to the presence of the cheating Mechanic.

These entail, quite simply, delivering the card with extra flourishes. A loud, "Here we go!", etc. (that covers up the "whishh"), often accompanied by raising the deck above the heads of the players. Sometimes the dealer must extend the elbows a bit, so as to get a proper grip on the cards. If you witness any of these actions during a game, and, in addition, they seem to take place during crucial periods of play, inevitably leading to disappointing results for the player, then, even if it's not happening to you, you should definitely sit up and take notice. I would advise leaving the game immediately.

I would *not* advise making accusations about cheating to the dealers or pit bosses. Barring the presence of your own video crew, you'll never be able to prove it. Furthermore, with the pressure being put on dealers in some casinos, who's to say that the dealer didn't take it upon her own volition to start dealing seconds?

Whatever you do, don't make a scene. There are proper channels to pursue for making complaints, including the executive offices of the casino, and the State Gaming Commission. Most of the loud complaints I've heard about cheating were from disgruntled losers or lousy players, often drunk. That's how it seemed, anyway. On the other hand, any written complaint must be followed up by an investigation, by the casino or commission, not that you'll necessarily hear anything about it. These things can add up, and too many written complaints won't bode well for any casino.

Now, back to the cheating Mechanic. Today's Mechanic isn't limited to the crudity of dealing herself an unknown second card. She isn't limited to helping only the casino, choosing instead, perhaps, to wait until some special friends come in, so they can scam the casino out of a pile of chips. Today's Mechanic can deal a known, predetermined card from any portion of the deck.

Some cards are even left in the deck face-up, until the time comes to deliver a bust card to you, or an ace to the dealer's blackjack. If she has to, she can always shuffle up before she gets to that upturned card.

The Amateur Mechanic.

As I've mentioned before, many of today's dealers are placed under enormous pressure to win for the casino. Those that do get the better shifts and the higher-paying tables. The losers get the worst hours and lower tips, a downward spiral that often ends up with firing or resignation. When the table starts losing is when you can most easily tell if the dealer is under pressure from the top.

The dealer's initial exclamations of congratulations to winners may tend to fade away if the winning continues. The dealer might seem to tense up or languish under the scrutiny of the pit boss. Attention from the pit may be worse on them than on the players, who are usually unaware of what's happening. The pit boss might whisper to her, "Who's winning?", and she may nod in your direction, perhaps answering cheerily, "He's doing pretty good!" Even without the pit boss's attention, a dealer who's under pressure may very well show nervousness when there are a lot of payouts.

From that point on, the dealer and the pit boss usually execute a pre-arranged set of defenses to stem the winning. This is usually the extent of the operation. But there may be a Mechanic called in, and not necessarily to cheat. Actually, you can win at a few tables and never see a Mechanic.

But sometimes, rarely, the dealer may feel like she's under so much pressure that she'll take matters into her own hands. She may try to claim a push as a loss for you, or call your win a push. Even more amateurish, she may "forget" to pay you, or underpay you. So, you should really pay attention to what's going on in front of you, just in case.

There's money lying around all over the place, and everybody wants some of it. The casino's trying to work the players, through alcohol and money-lust, into a state that they lose control over their wallets. At the same time, they insist that you practice self-control in the other aspects of your behavior.

Some of these casinos are not beyond cheating you out of your money. If you accuse them of it, they might just throw you out of the place. Fortunately, the practice of cheating customers is very limited. Most people don't even recognize it when it happens, and most of those that howl about being cheated, they're just bad losers.

Remember, the casinos are on the receiving end of an endless stream of thieves, con-artists, lock-pickers, chip-snatchers and general liars, all desperate to get their hands on that money, any way that they can. You can hardly blame the casinos for being rigid in their conduct.

It's unfortunate, however, when either the player or the casino adopts the attitude that they are at war with each other. It can only detract from the pleasure of, and lower the level of the game.

Chapter 11.

Six Ways to Improve Your Game Before You Ever Sit Down

(OR: HOW TO FIND A GOOD TABLE)

One: Don't sit down to a funeral. A somber, silent, unhappy table is usually a losing table. Often, there's one person resting his head in his hand (usually a male), fatalistically taking his losses. Winning tends to generate energy and happiness in players.

Caution: Make sure that it's not a table of drunks, happily throwing their money away. You'll see this sometimes.

Two: Take a glance at the dealer's chip tray. If it's a $5 table, are a lot of red chips gone? If a $25 table, are there many green chips gone? If you see a dealer receiving new chips, it *might* mean that she's been losing.

Caution: Even though there are chips gone, you may have already missed the winning session. Decks may have already been changed, as well.

Three: Look to see if the players have extra chips that they've won in front of them.

Caution: Watch out that they haven't just bought into the game, and just look like they've got a lot of chips, or, worse yet, have just bought more chips to replace losses.

Four: Look at the dealer's tips. A lot of tips may mean that the players have been winning. Some dealers collect tips in their shirt pocket; some keep them by the discards, or off to the side somewhere.

Caution: Some people tip even if they're losing, just to be nice, or in hopes of somehow turning their luck around.

Five: If the game seems hard to get into, determine why. Sometimes, in trying to keep a winning streak going, players will hang over the open chairs, or otherwise won't get out of your way to let you or anyone else into the game.

Caution: Some people are just rude slobs.

Six: Look where the pit bosses are watching. Their job includes keeping the dealers honest by watching the payouts. If they seem interested in a table, it may be because it's dropping money.

Caution: Pit bosses know this trick and may be sensitive to a player doing this. Also, just because they're looking at a table doesn't always mean that it's a winning table.

The Hit-and-Run.

There is a style of play known as Hitting-and-Running. By using the above tips or otherwise learning how to recognize a winning table, a good Hit-and-Run artist can end up in the plus column with very little effort applied. The down side is that they don't always get in a lot of playing time.

I practiced the Hit-and-Run successfully for quite a while, and I became quite sensitive to when a game was going well and when it started deteriorating. The problem arose when I was having too much fun playing and I didn't want to leave right away, even when the game was going downhill. Playing a game for lower stakes, just to get in playing time, wasn't a satisfactory solution, because there was always the temptation, especially during winning streaks, to make my bet larger.

The Hit-and-Run usually kept me in the black (in the winning column) as far as results went, and, when used properly, it has a number of good rationales behind it. But, as I've said earlier in the book, my game didn't become the powerful, balanced, long-term playing experience that it is today, until I discovered and blended in the CORE System with it.

With the CORE System I not only improved my winning percentage, from about 60–67% to all the way past 80%, but I increased the amount of eligible tables that I have to pick from. And, I've found that I'm able to play longer at any table I might pick. If the table is losing, I'm usually, at least, holding my own; if the rest of the table is just holding their own, then I'm almost inevitably winning. I get in all the playing time I want, at the betting level that I like best.

I've found the principles behind the CORE System to be sound, simple and powerful. As players around me curse or thank Lady Luck for their fortunes, I observe the mechanics of the Core consistently influencing theirs and my game.

By basing my strategy moves on the weight of the Core, I find myself making successful calls that don't fall into today's established patterns for the average player (including the Ten Counter, the Basic Strategist and the Shuffle Tracker). In so doing, I've sometimes managed to diffuse "heat" (suspicions from the dealers and/or the pit) aimed my direction while I continued to win, because my plays often make me look like I have no strategy at all, but am simply a lucky guy.

You don't need to learn all of the math. You only need

to learn the principles and correct strategy moves for the CORE System, and to recognize the trends that are occurring in front of you. Remember: "Trend" is where math overlaps with experience and intuition.

I now offer the CORE System to you.

Don't throw yourself to the mercies of Lady Luck. Take Luck into your own hands.

Appendix A

CORE Strategy Charts

These are the strategy charts for Hitting, Hard Doubles, Soft Doubles and Splitting. Each of these sections shows three charts. The middle, labeled "Normal Strategy," is the Basic Strategy, as devised by Thorp and Braun, for use with a balanced deck, or when the Core Count is zero. The left chart is for a Light Core, the right is for a Heavy Core.

Speaking for myself, I have not memorized every number on every chart. What I do is keep an informal count. I remain aware of whether the Core is Normal, Light or Heavy. If it's Light, I remain aware of whether it's slightly Light, fairly Light or extremely Light; if Heavy, then I watch to see if it's slightly Heavy, fairly Heavy or extremely Heavy. The more extreme the weight of the Core becomes, the more extreme are my deviations from Normal Strategy (the middle charts).

Remember "The Completion Principle." Ask yourself how well your hand and/or the dealer's hand combines with the Core cards, then determine the availability of those cards.

As far as the study of these charts goes, first learn the middle chart, then learn how the Light or Heavy Core changes the strategies shown in that middle chart. Look for patterns and trends, because a well-developed "feel" for the game is as good as a photographic memory.

NORMAL STRATEGY

Numbers indicate when to change from Normal Strategy; H becomes S; S becomes H.

Dark borders indicate Fringe Plays found on Table #6 & #7.

HITTING

	Dlr. Up Card									
Player Total:	2	3	4	5	6	7	8	9	T	A
17	S	S	S	S	S	S	S	S	S	S
16	S	S	S	S	S	S	H	H	H	H
15	S	S	S	S	S	S	H	H	H	H
14	S	S	S	S	S	S	H	H	H	H
13	S	S	S	S	S	S	H	H	H	H
12	H	H	S	S	S	H	H	H	H	H

Heavy CORE

	Dlr. Up Card									
	2	3	4	5	6	7	8	9	T	A
17	S	S	S	S	S	S	S	S	S	S
16	+8	+11	S	S	S	+8	+7	+16	H*	H
15	+8	+11	S	S	S	H	H	H	H	H
14	+4	+6	+8	+12	+14	H	H	H	H	H
13	+1	+2	+4	+6	+6	H	H	H	H	H
12	H	H	+1	+2	+2	H	H	H	H	H

*16 vs. Dlr. T: Hit except when count is only made up of fives.

Light CORE

	Dlr. Up Card									
	2	3	4	5	6	7	8	9	T	A
17	S	S	S	S	S	S	S	S	S	S
16	S	S	S	S	S	S	H	H	-16	-1-14
15	S	S	S	S	S	S	H	H	-12	-4-10
14	S	S	S	S	S	S	H	H	-10	-5
13	S	S	S	S	S	S	H	H	-14-14	-10-7-10
12	S	-3-2	S	S	S	S	H	H	H	-14-15

HARD DOUBLES

	Dlr. Up Card									
	2	3	4	5	6	7	8	9	T	A
11	D	D	D	D	D	D	D	D	D	D*
10	D	D	D	D	D	D	D	D	H	H
9	H	D	D	D	D	H	H	H	H	H
8	H	H	H	H	H	H	H	H	H	H
7	H	H	H	H	H	H	H	H	H	H

Two Card Hand:

Heavy CORE

	Dlr. Up Card									
	2	3	4	5	6	7	8	9	T	A
11	D	+12	+12	+15	D	D	D	D+12	+6	+1
10	+12	+12	+15	D	D-5	D-5	+13	+4	H	H
9	H	+2	+4	+8	+16	D-16	H	H	H	H
8	H	H	H	H	H	H	H	H	H	H
7	H	H	H	H	H	H	H	H	H	H

Light CORE

	Dlr. Up Card									
	2	3	4	5	6	7	8	9	T	A
11	D	D	D	D	D	D	D	D	D	-1
10	D	D	D	D	D	D	D	D	-4	-4
9	-1	D	D	D	D	D-12	H	H	H	H
8	H	-13	-8	-8	-8	H§	H	H	H	H
7	H	H	H	H	H	H	H	H	H	H

NORMAL STRATEGY

*11 vs. Dlr. A: Hit when Dlr. stands on Soft 17.

Numbers indicate changes from Normal Strategy. D becomes H; H becomes D.

Dark borders indicate Fringe Plays found on Table #8.

§8 vs. Dlr. 6: Double if −2 count is made of fives only, otherwise, always Hit.

SOFT DOUBLES

Heavy CORE

Dlr. Up Card

	2	3	4	5	6	7	8	9	T	A
A,9	S	S	S	S	S	S	S	S	S	S
A,8	S	S	S	S	S	S	S	S	S	S
A,7	S	S	+2	+3	+6	+7	S	S	+10	+8
A,6	H	H	H	+2	+8	H	H	H	H	H
A,5	H	H	H	+2	+10	D	H	H	H	H
A,4	H	H	H	+8	+14	D	H	H	H	H
A,3	H	H	H	+2	+10	D	D	H	H	H
A,2	H	H	H	D	D	H	H	H	H	H

Dark borders indicate Fringe Plays shown on Table # 9.

Two Card Hand

Dlr. Up Card

	2	3	4	5	6	7	8	9	T	A
A,9	S	S	S	S	S	S	S	S	S	S
A,8	S	S	S	S	S	S	S	S	S	S
A,7	S	S	S	D	D	S*	S	S	H	H
A,6	H	D	D	D	D	H	H	H	H	H
A,5	H	H	D	D	D	H	H	H	H	H
A,4	H	H	D	D	D	H	H	H	H	H
A,3	H	H	H	D	D	H	H	H	H	H
A,2	H	H	H	D	D	H	H	H	H	H

NORMAL STRATEGY

*A,8 vs. Dlr.6: Double when dealer hits soft 17.

For hands A,6 and lower numbers indicate changes from D to H; H to D.

For hands A,7 and higher numbers indicate chanes from S to D; D to S.

Light CORE

Dlr. Up Card

	2	3	4	5	6	7	8	9	T	A
A,9	-12	-11	-12	-13	-14	S	S	S	S	S
A,8	-9	-6	-7	-4	-3	S	S	S	S	H
A,7	-1	D	D	D	D	-12	-12	S	H	H
A,6	-1	D	D	D	D	-7	H	H	H	H
A,5	-7	a2	D	D	D	D	H	H	H	H
A,4	-12	-11	e5	D	D	D	H	H	H	H
A,3	H	-14	-15	b12	b8	H	H	H	H	H
A,2	H	H	aH	c4	D	H	H	H	H	H

a-A,5 vs. Dlr. 3: Hit if CORE Count is fives only.

b-A,3 vs. Dlr. 5 & 6: Hit if CORE Count is sevens only.

c-A,2 vs. Dlr. 6: Double if CORE Count is fives only.

d-A,2 & A,8 vs Dlr. 5: Double if CORE Count is only fives and/or sixes.

e-A,4 vs Dlr 4: Double if CORE Count is sevens only.

f-A,8 vs. Dlr 6: Stand if CORE Count is eights only.

¶NOTE: You're already going to win the majority of your soft nineteens and twenties. If, however you still wish to risk it, here are the counts for the bes changes. As shown, conditions must be extreme to make it worthwhile.

SPLITTING

Normal Strategy (Player Pairs)

Player Pair	2	3	4	5	6	7	8	9	T	A
9,9	P	P	P	P	P	S	P	P	S	S
8,8	P	P	P	P	P	P	P	P	P	P
7,7	P	P	P	P	P	S	H	H	H	H
6,6	H	P	P	P	S	H	H	H	H	H
4,4	H	H	H	P	P	H	H	H	H	H
3,3	H	H	P	P	P	P	H	H	H	H
2,2	H	H	P	P	P	P	P	H	H	H
A,A	P	P	P	P	P	P	P	P	P	P

NORMAL STRATEGY

Numbers indicate changes from Normal Strategy;

P becomes H; H becomes P, except Light CORE (6,6), where numbers indicate to stand and for (9,9), where P becomes S; S becomes P.

Light CORE

	2	3	4	5	6	7	8	9	T	A
9,9	P	P	P	P	P	-6	P	P	S	-7
8,8	P	P	P	P	P	P	P	P	-7	-12
7,7	P	P	P	P	P	S	H	-7	H	H
6,6	-1	P	P	P	P	S	b-6	H	H	H
4,4	H	H	H	P	P	H	H	H	H	H
3,3	H	Hc	P	P	P	P	-3	H	H	H
2,2	H	H	P	P	d-6	P	P	H	H	H
A,A	P	P	P	P	P	P	P	P	P	P

a-(6,6) vs. Dlr. 2: Unless that one (or two) card(s) is five(s).

b-(6,6) vs. Dlr. 7: Unless two or more cards are fives.

c-(3,3) vs. Dlr. 3: Unless CORE Count is five only.

d-(2,2) vs. Dlr. 7: Unless CORE Count is eights only.

Heavy CORE

	2	3	4	5	6	7	8	9	T	A
9,9	+3	+3	+6	+7	+8	S	+6	+7	S	S
8,8	P	P	P	P	P	P	S	P	P	P
7,7	+6	+6	S	S	S	P	H	H	H	H
6,6	H	+1	+3	S	+15	H	H	H	H	H
4,4	H	H	H	H	H	H	H	H	H	H
3,3	H	P	P	P	P	+4	+8	+11	+9	
2,2	H	+2	+2	+2	+2	P	P	H	H	H
A,A	P	P	P	P	P	P	P	+12	+10	+7

e-(4,4) vs. Dlr. 6: +10 when Dlr. hits soft 17.

f-(2,2) vs. Dlr. 3,4,5: Unless you've seen no eights.

Appendix B

Surrender.

Some casinos offer the "Surrender" play. If the player so desires he may, before taking hits or making any other play, "surrender" half his bet rather than losing it all by playing out the hand.

"Late Surrender" originated in foreign casinos. With it, a player may give up a hand containing any number of cards, plus only half his bet, provided his hand doesn't exceed twenty-one and the dealer doesn't show an ace.

"Early Surrender," as introduced in 1978 by Resorts International, Atlantic City, entails the opportunity to surrender the original two card hand and half the wager *before* the dealer checks for blackjack.

Julian Braun, blackjack's leading computer expert, has calculated a .064% (read that, 64 thousands of 1%) player advantage with a blanket policy of surrender in these situations:

T,6 and 7,9 vs. Dlr. T or A

T,5 and 6,9 vs. Dlr. T

In other words, as a blanket policy, it plays an insignificant role.

However, in my opinion, surrender in these situations (all four of which occur a total of roughly once in every twenty-two hands), can become a significant move if you've noticed that the deck is in the midst of a strong

Ten Clump. This greatly increases the chance for a dealer twenty or blackjack, as well as for a hit to bust you.

Therefore, in facing the Defensive Deck, I would advise "Surrender" on the aforementioned plays only if you have a sense that you're in the presence of a strong Ten Clump.

Insurance.

For those that don't wish to bother with Insurance, they can do what I did for years, which is *never insure.* The 2–1 payoff for insuring when dealer has a blackjack doesn't equal the actual odds that you're betting on (as with virtually all casino bets).

Actual odds are 13–4, or $3\frac{1}{4}$–1, that the dealer will have a ten in the hole at any given time. Those that take "even money" on their blackjacks whenever they see a dealer ace, instead of the normal 3–2 payoff, are really losing money in the long run. ("Even money" means that, in effect, you've insured your blackjack.)

But for those that develop a good eye for Ten Clumps, insurance can become another matter.

Insurance, for those of you unsure of how it operates, is a 2–1 bet that the casino offers whenever the dealer up card is an ace. Before any other play continues, a player may bet *up to* (but not necessarily only) 50% of their original wager on the chance that the dealer has a ten in the hole for a blackjack. After asking who, if anyone, wants to take insurance, the dealer then looks at her hole card. If she has the ten, for blackjack, everyone loses their original wager (except for an uninsured player blackjack, which pushes). Then the house pays off at 2–1 any insurance bets taken. If the dealer has something other than a ten in the hole, all insurance bets are lost and play continues as normal.

Players tend to insure higher hands, but if you're dealt a T,T, for twenty, in a one- or two-deck game, remember that you're holding two tens that can't be in the dealer's hole.

My advice is, if you want to play the insurance game, then play it only when you believe that you're in a strong clump of Tens, and then only if you have a decent hand—nineteen or up, or a hard eleven that can hit for a ten from the same clump (with a Light Core, of course!)

If you have a high, hard stiff, fifteen or sixteen (not 8,8, though), the Surrender option will be the better move, in the presence of a strong Ten Clump.

You can become a very successful player without *ever* considering surrender or insurance. The converse of this, always insuring anything, would penalize your game by only .23 of 1%. On the other hand, if you always stood on stiffs vs. dealer high cards, you'd lose an additional 3% of your hands. Always hitting vs. dealer small cards costs you another 3.2%. Never doubling down costs another 1.6%. You'll lose 7.8 extra hands per 100 by not playing your basic hitting, standing and doubling game properly. But, if you always insure and never surrender, you won't even cost yourself .4 of one hand per 100, in the long run.*

A person can play without ever thinking about surrendering, and never taking insurance, and be a highly successful player. So, save these fine touches for when you're already a winner. Then, make your decisions based on the presence or absence of Ten Clumps.

---

*Figures taken from Griffin's *Theory of Blackjack,* p. 150, "The World's Worst Blackjack Player."

Appendix C

DEALER'S FINAL TOTAL PROBABILITIES

(When Dealer Doesn't Have Blackjack)

Dealer Up Card	17 or 18	19 or More	Bust
2	28	37	35
3	27	36	37
4	25	35	40
5	24	34	42
6	27	31	42
7	51	23	26
8	49	27	24
9	24	53	23
T	24	53	23
A	37	46	17
% Overall:	29.84	41.08	29.08

[When there's no Blackjack]

Glossary

ACTIVE HAND: Any hand that has the option of adding another card to its total, provided that the original total is less than hard 17. (Opposite: Standing Hand)

BASIC STRATEGY: A traditional method of play, first computerized by Julian Braun in the 1960s, by which, through millions of computer-played hands, the most mathematically advantageous response is provided for every player/dealer hand combination, based on the assumption that the deck is random.

BUST: Or Break. When either the player or dealer hand total goes over twenty-one, which causes the hand to lose.

CHEQUE: Another, more official word for betting chip.

CLUMP: A group of cards of like or similar value, grouped together in one part of a deck or shoe. A clump may or may not contain a few cards of unsimilar value within it.

COMPLETION PRINCIPLE: The concept of the availability, in the remaining deck, of cards which will enable a hand, on the next hit, to reach the totals of twenty or twenty-one. The presence or absence of these cards is the most important consideration of the game, second only to the potential of the deck to provide a good initial, two-card hand.

COUNTING: Or Card Tracking. The use of any system to calculate the surplus or deficit of certain cards in a remaining deck. The systems vary greatly, but generally assign values to the cards so that the complete deck adds up to zero. (Example: 2–6 = +1; 7–9 = 0; T–A = −1) These systems are easily defeated by casinos. (Card Counter: A player that uses a counting system.)

DEFENSIVE DECK: Any of the decks or shoes created by casinos, containing certain card structures designed to offset advantages gained by the player's use of some combination of traditional Basic Strategy, Ten Tracking and Plus/Minus Card Counting. While more than one version of the Defensive Deck exists, some more complex than others, they all depend on some type of card clumping.

DOUBLE DOWN: When the house permits, a player may announce that they wish to "double down" on their two card hand, placing out another wager equal to their original wager, and receiving one card, face down. Some houses allow doubling only on ten or eleven, others on ten, eleven and soft hands, while others, on any first two cards. In addition, a few places will allow doubling down after a split.

FRINGE PLAY: Any of the player/dealer hand combinations whose strategy responses are the first to be affected by Core imbalances.

HIT: To ask for and receive another card, or, as a noun, the additional card itself. A player may hit as many times as they wish, as long as they don't go over twenty-one. The two exceptions to this are doubling down, when you receive only one card and splitting aces, when you receive only one card on each ace.

HIT-AND-RUN: A method of play that involves (usually brief) games at a number of tables, often, but not necessarily, based on some criteria that the player believes indicates that each table is ready to provide winning hands upon his arrival.

HOLE CARD: The dealer's face-down card.

MECHANIC: A "recovery artist" for the house, usually called in to help a dropping table turn back to the house. Generally a more experienced dealer, often utilizing more sophisticated defensive measures. A Mechanic is not necessarily a cheater.

NATURAL: Another name for a blackjack.

PIT: An area of the casino that offers a certain game, such as the Blackjack Pit. Also, the restricted, enclosed area formed by the layout of the tables, allowing access only to casino personnel.

PUSH: A tie between dealer and player, occurring when both hands have the same total. No money is won or lost.

REAL RATIO: (Core Ratio) Used in multi-deck games, it is the reduction of the Core Count as it would apply to one deck. All of the Core Strategy Charts are written for one deck.

Formula: (# of surplus [+] or deficit [−] Core cards × 4) ÷ (# of ¼ decks remaining.)

SETTLEMENT: The determination of the highest total between player and dealer hands, and the resulting payoff, loss or keeping (in event of a tie) of the wager.

SHILL: An employee of the house who plays at the table and attempts to make decisions that will favor the house. Also, a player for the house that is simply trying to draw other players into a game, this last sometimes known as a "starter."

SPLIT: When a player is dealt a pair, he has the option of "splitting" them. The cards are separated and an additional, equal wager is put up. Then each card takes hits and is played as a separate hand. The first hand must be completed before the second can be played. If the same denomination is received on the first hit, the house may allow an additional split (a "resplit"), if desired. Most houses limit the amount of splits for any one hand to four. The player may take as many hits as desired, except when splitting Aces, when only one hit per Ace is allowed. Some houses will, in addition, allow a player to double down on a split hand.

SPREAD: or Betting Ratio. The betting spread is the limits between the lowest and highest wagers made by a bettor during a game. Often spoken of in ratios, a spread of $10 to $50 would be a 5:1 ratio, or a 5:1 spread.

SOFT HAND: Any hand, containing any number of cards, in which an ace may be counted as one or eleven.

STAND: When a player desires no more cards, or no cards at all, they announce that they wish to "Stand" on their hand.

STANDING HAND: Traditionally refers to any hand totaling hard seventeen through twenty-one, in part, because the dealer cannot hit again with these totals and, also, because a player generally won't hit these totals.

STIFF: Any hand that has the potential to break, or total twenty-two or more on the next hit. Stiffs are comprised of the totals of hard twelve through sixteen.

TOKE: A tip, or gratuity, for the dealer or other employees, as in "Toking the dealer."

TRAVELER'S CHEQUE: A betting chip that rolls on its side across the table.

UNIT: An easy way to think of bets, as in "size of betting unit" or number of units won or lost. It is the amount of the basic, average wager made when the player believes that the strategic situation is neutral.